NEW BEGINNINGS

New Beginnings

Preparing Families for Remarriage in the Church

GORDON E. ELLIS

THE PILGRIM PRESS

New York

Unless otherwise noted, scripture quotations are from *The New English Bible*, © by The Delegates of the Oxford University Press and The Syndics of the Cambridge University Press 1961, 1970 and are used by permission. Quotations marked "RSV" are from the Revised Standard Version of the Bible, copyrighted 1946, 1952, © 1971, 1973 by the Division of Christian Education of the National Council of the Churches of Christ in the U.S.A., and are used by permission. The quotation identified as "Phillips" is from *Letters to Young Churches* (New York: Macmillan Co., 1948).

Cover Design by Ed Carenza

Library of Congress Cataloging-in-Publication Data

Ellis, Gordon E.
    New beginnings : preparing families for remarriage in the church / Gordon E. Ellis.
        p.   cm.
    Includes bibliographical references.
    ISBN 0-8298-0896-5
    1. Remarried people—Pastoral counseling of.   2. Divorced people—Pastoral counseling of. 3. Remarriage—Religious aspects—Christianity. 4. Church work with families.   I. Title.
    BV4012.27E45   1991
    259'.1—dc20   91-9640
                                                                                         CIP

Printed in the United States of America.
10 9 8 7 6 5 4 3 2 1

The Pilgrim Press, 475 Riverside Drive, New York, NY 10115

To my parents
Frederick and Helen Ellis
who instilled in me a love for learning
and helped me immeasurably in making
this dream a reality

Contents

Dedication   *v*

Acknowledgments   *ix*

Preface   *xi*

Chapter One   Remarriage in the Church
                   Following Divorce?   *1*

Chapter Two   Is It Faithful to the Gospel?   *11*

Chapter Three   Preparing Families for Remarriage
                   in the Church: A Model Process   *19*

Chapter Four   Session 1: Building the Foundation   *29*

Chapter Five   Session 2: Looking at Yesterday
                   and Today with the Couple   *39*

Chapter Six   Session 3: Looking Ahead
                   with the Couple   *51*

Chapter Seven   The Counseling Process with the
                   Children   *63*

Chapter Eight   Session 4: Creating
                   the Remarriage Ceremony   *77*

Chapter Nine   Conclusion   *91*

List of Works Cited   *95*

Suggestions for Further Study   *97*

Appendix   My Parent Is Getting Remarried:
                   A Workbook to Help Children Prepare
                   for the Remarriage of a Parent   *103*

Acknowledgments

Without the assistance of some wonderful people, this book might not have been possible. I am grateful to each and every one. My wife, Diane, and our children, Ryan and Lyndsey, have supported and encouraged me throughout, often sacrificing their own wants and needs so that I could complete the book. My parents, Helen and Frederick Ellis, to whom this book is dedicated, have offered endless hours of clerical assistance, grammatical expertise, and proofreading. My doctoral adviser, Dr. Miriam Therese Winter, has been a constant source of strength and motivation. I am also indebted to the faculty of Hartford Seminary, who encouraged me to publish my work; to Pilgrim Press for publishing a first-time author; and to my editor, Harold Twiss, for his assistance in transforming a doctoral dissertation into a book.

The love, support, and sacrifice provided by the Seekonk Congregational Church, United Church of Christ, family was amazing. I am especially thankful for the selfless hard work of my partner in ministry there, the Reverend Joy C. Utter; the professional clerical assistance and concerned "listening" of Patricia Jennings; the leadership skills of Carolyn (Waller) Bradley, who expanded my bibliography, monitored my "mental health," and led the church in ministering to my needs; the quiet "haven" for work and study provided me by Wilt and Elsie Pierce; the ministry of love provided by the two children's counselors, Judy Provost and Laura Riggs-Mitchell; and the extra work of secretary Janice Moran.

Two friends, Cheryl Cabral and Dorothy Levesque, are appreciated for their professional assistance and imagination in the early phases of my work. I also thank the many others who offered loving support and kindness during the five years of my doctoral work as well as during the writing of this book: Russell and Lillian Deane, Rick and Sherry (Deane) Briggs, Connie Keene, Daehler Hayes, my clergy support group colleagues Bill Cabell, George Peters, Dick Anderston, Brian Ladr, and Catherine Cadieux, and my new church family at the First Congregational Church of Southington, Connecticut.

I am also grateful to the many families who participated in my doctoral project, out of which this book was born. Thank you for sharing with me your hopes and dreams, fears and frustrations, goals, growing edges, feelings, and struggles. You have given me the most precious gift that anyone can offer to another human being: You have allowed me to enter your lives, minister to you, learn from you, and share my learnings in this book. I have masked your names and identities to protect your privacy.

Finally, and most of all, I thank God, to whose glory my ministry and this book are offered.

GORDON E. ELLLIS

Preface

Some people noted after reading my doctoral dissertation that they thought during a significant portion of it that I must be working through my feelings regarding my own divorce and remarriage. They were surprised to read in the conclusion that I have been neither divorced nor remarried, and that I live happily with my first and only wife and two children. Moreover, I have had no one in my close family experience divorce or remarry. Instead, my interest in this important issue grew out of my ministry at the Seekonk Congregational Church, United Church of Christ, Seekonk, Massachusetts.

Many times each year I receive requests to remarry people who have experienced divorce. Often they are people who have felt "turned away" by their own churches and come in hopes of finding a church that will allow them an opportunity to stand at the altar once again for a Christian wedding. Prior to embarking on the research contained in this book, I felt increasingly uncomfortable about my theological position regarding divorce and remarriage, as well as about my ignorance concerning the unique kinds of families that result from remarriage. I knew that I was not preparing people adequately for what would lie ahead, not using the occasion of the remarriage ceremony itself to its fullest potential. By the time I was choosing a focus for my doctor of ministry project at Hartford Seminary, this was one of the most pressing issues in my ministry. The results of my work are contained on the pages that follow.

Not only has this work increased my sensitivity and competence as a minister, but it has also made our family more compassionate, sensitive, and understanding in our dealings with the many stepfamilies around us. (One in five children in our children's school, and more than one in three children in their church school, live in stepfamilies.) I hope that this book will benefit other pastors, counselors, and their families as much.

Before they attempt to use this remarriage preparation process, I urge pastors and counselors to read this volume through thoroughly and, if possible, to read some of the work suggested for further study listed at the end of the book. Please note that there are several resources on which this project depends: one handout, two audiotapes about stepfamily living, a children's workbook, and children's book. The handout and the children's workbook are included in this volume and can be reproduced inexpensively and easily. The audiotapes and children's book must be ordered prior to starting the process. Chapter 3 offers details about acquiring these resources.

My hope and prayer is that this will be a welcome, useful, and effective tool for pastors and counselors who prepare families for remarriage. More importantly, however, I hope it benefits those adults and children who are entering stepfamilies, that they might find the new life and faith that remarriage in the church can offer.

NEW BEGINNINGS

CHAPTER ONE

Remarriage in the Church Following Divorce?

As Todd knelt in prayer beside his new wife, Brenda, their hands joined in prayer with the hands of his two new stepsons, tears began streaming down his cheeks. Seeing the depth of his emotions, Brenda and her two boys also started to cry their own tears of joy and hope. So much emotion then swept over the sanctuary that even the minister had trouble reading the lines of the pastoral prayer that he had penned for the remarriage ceremony of this family which had so recently endured the agony of each spouse's divorce. It was a scene reminiscent of that evening at Simon's house, described so beautifully in Luke 7:36–50, when the woman washed Jesus' feet with her tears and dried them with her hair. The healing touch of God's love and forgiveness was being felt; new life was being received.

Unfortunately, scenes such as this are all too rare today in the Christian churches of America. It is not usually compassion that is lacking, however, but an inability to deal with the dilemma in which the church finds itself. On the one hand, the church exists in a culture with a high rate of divorce. Figures from the United States Department of Health and Human Services point out that the number of divorces in relation to the number of marriages in the United

States increased almost steadily between 1900, when there was one divorce for every 12.7 marriages, and 1980, when one divorce occurred for every two marriages. In contrast, these words of Jesus concerning divorce and remarriage are firm and haunting: "What God has joined together, man must not separate" (Matthew 19:6) and "A man who divorces his wife and marries another commits adultery; and anyone who marries a woman divorced from her husband commits adultery" (Luke 16:18).

It is not only the rate of divorce that puts the Christian church in a difficult position, but also the ever-increasing number of couples and families coming to the church requesting to be remarried.

> Divorce apparently does not sour most people on marriage. The vast majority of divorced people remarry. In fact, 83 percent of all divorced men and 75 percent of all divorced women remarry. Remarriages are so popular they constitute 30 percent of all marriages performed annually. (Grunlan 1984, p. 331)

These figures have been verified in my ministry. Over fourteen years of ministry, I have officiated at 121 wedding ceremonies, 57 of which were remarriages for one or both partners. Moreover, within the congregation where this process for remarriage preparation was created, the Seekonk Congregational Church, United Church of Christ, in Seekonk, Massachusetts, 22 percent of the 410 adult members live in families born out of remarriage following divorce, as do 34 percent of the 203 children under the age of seventeen. Statistics such as these indicate that the issues of divorce and remarriage are increasing in magnitude today. This is due primarily to shifting values within our society, where fewer than 10 percent of the households are what we once called "the typical American family," with Mom at home, Dad working, and two or more kids. Today more woman are in the work force; traditional lines of authority are being challenged; there is more concern for individualism and self-fulfillment; and alternative lifestyles are becoming increasingly more acceptable. In addition, as a publication of the Family Service America states:

> The persisting high divorce rate and the richness of family structures suggest that perhaps value shifts and other changes in society are cre-

ating expectations for the family much higher than those held by previous generations. Sharing, intimacy, and emotional support are set
at too high a level of expectation to be sustained by many people form-
ing families. But for those who do succeed, the quality of family life
at such high levels is immeasurably superior to the more constrained
family models of an earlier age when less was expected and less was
achieved. Family Service America, 1984, p. 10)

This "quality over quantity" mentality and other cultural value
shifts, combined with a rise in secularism and pluralism in the
United States that has weakened the traditional authority of the
church in such matters, have contributed to these high and increasing statistics for divorce and remarriage.

These figures pose a difficult dilemma for the church in America.
While desiring and being called upon to respond pastorally to families experiencing divorce and remarriage, the church must also be
faithful to Jesus, whose words cited above, as well as those in Mark
10:1–12, Matthew 19:1–12, and Matthew 5:31–32, show his obvious strong bias against divorce and remarriage. Are these the actual
words of Jesus or the work of later biblical editors? If Jesus did
speak them, what was his intent, and what are the implications for
the church today? Should the church take a public stand regarding
divorce and remarriage? If so, how lenient or severe should it be?
Should members of the clergy officiate at remarriage ceremonies?
Can divorced and remarried people receive the sacraments of the
church and hold positions of leadership within it? These questions,
and a multitude of others, are being asked in and of the church
today with an intensity that increases along with the divorce and
remarriage statistics. Moreover, how the church responds not only
affects Christians today, but also will have profound effect on
Christians in America, as well as the church itself, well into the next
century. With researchers predicting that nearly half of today's children will not live continuously with both biological parents, it is
important to realize that a significant portion of tomorrow's church
members are being affected by divorce and remarriage. They will not
forget how the church ministers to their needs today.

Unfortunately, there has been very little consensus in the church
regarding the issues of divorce and remarriage. Citing Jesus' state-

ments in the Synoptic Gospels to justify a strong opposition to divorce and remarriage, as well as a subtle, and sometimes obvious, pastoral discrimination against people who have experienced them, is one prevalent response within the church. Sandra, a Roman Catholic, who had divorced her husband after enduring his abusive behavior for ten years, wrote: "After being rejected by the Catholic Church, I felt quite negative, since it seemed that I was being punished for a crime that I had not committed." Some denominations and individual members of the clergy, however, with various degrees of comfort or discomfort, have tended to be more accepting of divorce and remarriage.

What this lack of agreement in the church has meant, at a practical level, is that couples seeking remarriage most often receive from the church either judgment, silence, or uncomfortable participation. These responses very often increase the feelings of guilt with which they and their families already tend to be struggling. Therefore, such couples usually search out either civil authorities or the most flexible and uncritical ministers and churches, who out of ignorance or discomfort very often treat these unique marriages as if they were first marriages. Without adequate preparation for the complex dynamics of living as a stepfamily, and without assistance in the difficult task of building bonds between parents, stepparents, children, and stepchildren, newly remarried families are at high risk to face yet another divorce:

> Forty percent of second marriages end in divorce within the first four years. Another ten to fifteen percent are stable but unhappy. The poor record seems largely due to 1) lack of preparation, 2) unrealistic expectations, and 3) poor communication. (O'Brien and O'Brien 1983, p. xiii)

Remarriages are very different from first marriages. Therefore, if clergy and churches do decide to participate in them, the preparation process must take the differences seriously. The first and most important difference is implied in the fact that families created out of remarriages have traditionally been called "stepfamilies." The term "step" derives from an Old English prefix, "steop," meaning "bereaved" or "orphaned." Thus, the new family is created out of loss, and the pain that always accompanies loss. Moreover, the loss is multifaceted. All marriages are entered with hopes and dreams, visions and promises, which offer great joy, excitement, and happiness to the spouses. When a marriage ends, each partner not only loses a spouse, often a lifestyle, and sometimes frequent contact with the children; but he or she also faces the death of these important hopes and dreams.

To enter into a new marriage without resolving the grief and pain of divorce is to ensure that the new relationship will be complicated by the unresolved feelings and conflicts from the earlier one. Further complicating this new relationship is the fact that usually in remarriage situations it is not only the couple themselves who carry this grief and pain with them, but also their children. Children, in fact, are less likely to have completed the mourning process, and may well view the remarriage of their parent as yet another loss rather than a gain. Helping adults and children grieve and find healing must be an essential element in any counseling process that prepares them for remarriage. Sandra, the divorced Catholic who wrote of her anger at the church, included in the same letter to me following her family's remarriage preparation: "Dealing with you helped me to separate the 'rules' of a particular church from 'religion' in general. I was angry and disappointed with the humans who dictated the rules, not with God. Your attitude toward remarriage is like that which I might expect from God, accepting, forgiving, and helpful."

A second difference between remarriage and first marriage is that people entering remarriages following divorce tend to have feelings of guilt regarding the breakdown of their past marriages. The intensity of this guilt varies depending on each individual's values, religious background, and responsibility in the various causes of the breakup. Again, it is not just the couple who carry these guilt feelings, but invariably the children as well. Children, especially younger children, usually overestimate their own power, and very often assume that they somehow have control over the people and situations around them. Therefore, they often assume responsibility for actions and events, even when nothing could be farther from the truth.

Part of people's preparation for remarriage involves talking about and resolving these guilt feelings. Discussing whether or not they are legitimate feelings can alleviate some of those which are not. Others, however, can only be resolved by a pronouncement of absolution, which, of course, is part of the church's work as the body of Christ. We are the present-day recipients of the charge that the risen Christ gave to his disciples: "'As the Father sent me, so I send you.' Then he breathed on them, saying, 'Receive the Holy Spirit! If you forgive any man's sins, they stand forgiven'" (John 20: 21–22).

The third difference of remarriage after divorce from first marriage, like the previous two, results from the very fact that it is preceded by divorce. Generally people entering stepfamilies, both adults and children, enter carrying more emotional "baggage" than just feelings of loss and guilt. This "baggage" invariably affects the new relationship, usually in a negative way. Preparing the adults and children involved for remarriage means dealing openly with and resolving as many emotions as possible, so that their emotional state mirrors their legal status. In this way, the effects of their previous relationships on their new one can be kept to a minimum. Achieving emotional divorce is more difficult than obtaining a legal divorce. It usually takes three to five years, in fact.

Another difference is the children themselves. Many, if not most, remarriages involve children from previous marriages. These may be children who will live in the new household created by the remarriage, children who will visit on an occasional or regular basis, children who are no longer actively involved in their parents' lives, grown children, young children, or any combination of these. Since children are the primary cause for divorce after remarriage, their presence, needs, and feelings must be taken as seriously as those of their parent and stepparent. Some of the issues that must be discussed in preparation for remarriage are the children's living and visitation arrangements, their feelings about the remarriage and the soon-to-be stepparent, their relationship with stepsiblings, changes in their roles and functions in the new family (and maybe even their place in the birth order), potential loyalty conflicts between their biological parents and their stepparents, and many more. The children present many complex issues, which obviously cannot all be resolved within the scope of a remarriage preparation process. However, assisting the family in the development of a positive and healthy communication style, as well as in learning good negotiation techniques, can provide an important foundation upon which they can continue to work through these and future problems more efficiently and effectively as they arise. This goal can be achieved in the preparation process. As one couple, Tom and Sarah, and her two children found out:

> The talking—between Tom and me, the children and us—was a healing process. Neither of us were used to communication. None of our previous relationships had communication. You made us open up, speak honestly, and bare those feelings we've kept hidden for a lot of years. More importantly, you taught us *how* to communicate so that even now, we try not to hide our feelings from each other. It's made a world of difference in our relationship.

Another extremely important difference between first marriage and remarriage is that in a remarriage, instead of two people bringing together their own unique backgrounds, values, expectations, roles, and the like, two families are being merged, quite often with many people involved. This means that a stepfamily can never function like a natural, biological family, even though most people assume that it will. Preparing families for remarriage involves helping them relinquish this myth and begin the process of deciding what from their past will be kept, what discarded, and what blended. As these decisions are made, and compromises ironed out, a new family begins to emerge, and its members begin to feel part of it.

For all these reasons and many more, remarriages are very different from first marriages, and, therefore, the preparation process also needs to be different. The process offered in the following chapters takes these differences into account. It attempts to provide a healing, loving, life-giving, and faithful tool for ministry with families entering remarriage, a tool that will help pastors and others prepare such families for the unique difficulties and opportunities of remarriage and stepfamily living.

Before we examine how the church can offer such a ministry while remaining faithful to the words of Jesus in the Gospels regarding divorce and remarriage, it should be noted that the process presented in this book may be more time-consuming than the preparation procedures that pastors and others presently use. It is worth the time, however, for several reasons.

First, it is needed. The high rate of divorce after remarriage says a great deal about the need for better remarriage preparation.

Second, many pastors spend a great deal of time counseling stepfamilies around issues that might have been resolved as part of a good remarriage preparation process. The process suggested here would eliminate at least some of that time.

Third, it provides the church with an opportunity to offer individuals and families a beautiful example of the relevant and life-promoting resurrection faith that is our good news to share, while at the same time ministering to the needs of our society by helping to build stronger families. This is especially important since many families seeking remarriage have had very negative experiences with the church regarding their divorce and/or remarriage and often come with angry, even hostile feelings. Taking them seriously, meeting their needs, and developing bonds with them can enhance their relationship with the church, and even with God, and potentially increase their involvement in the life of the church. Of all the remarriages I have performed in which neither spouse was previously involved in my church, two thirds of those families have since become involved to a significant degree.

Fourth, many ministers and counselors are delighted to find out, as I have, that such persons tend to be much more highly motivated than first-marrieds to confront and work on areas of concern and conflict in their relationship, as well as to explore the unique joys and challenges facing them as they become a family unit. They also tend to be more dedicated to the survival of the new marriage and family than they were to their previous one, and willing to do whatever is necessary to ensure its survival.

Finally, statistics verify that a good remarriage preparation process does indeed help build stronger stepfamilies. In fact, in tests at the Step Family Foundation in New York, out of the five hundred couples counseled prior to remarriage, only four went on to divorce (Francke 1983, p. 209).

It is essential that couples, and even entire families, learn what they can expect in a stepfamily and how they can communicate, negotiate, and interact in ways that will enhance the strength and cohesiveness of their new family.

Because many people desiring to be remarried feel strongly about the importance of being married in the church, even in a denomination different from that with which they normally are affiliated, the church has a unique opportunity to help these families as they prepare for remarriage. In fact, this may be one of the most needed and important ministries that the church can provide to American families today. But is it faithful to the gospel?

CHAPTER TWO

Is It Faithful to the Gospel?

Divorce and remarriage are not new issues for Americans. In fact, the remarriage rate in the United States in the 1970s and 1980s paralleled the remarriage rate in the United States and Europe in the seventeenth and eighteenth centuries. It was, however, death rather than divorce that caused the high rate of remarriage in that earlier era. Remarriage was, therefore, much more socially acceptable, and in some cases even expected. For example, in Plimouth Plantation in colonial America, if a widowed person with children was unable to remarry within about six months following the death of a spouse, the magistrate assigned a new spouse to that person, and a remarriage ceremony took place. Remarriage following divorce, however, has never been as well received, and despite its present prevalence it still is not, especially in the church.

Divorce and remarriage are not new issues for the church either. A Roman Catholic Church historian and theologian, Theodore Mackin, S.J., published an important volume in 1984 entitled *Divorce and Remarriage.* In it, he carefully traces, century by century, the cultural trends in regard to these issues as well as the church's response to these trends, noting that as far back as the Roman Empire, even in the years before and during Jesus' life, as well as during the development of the early church, divorce and remarriage were commonplace. The laws of the Roman Empire, of which Israel in Jesus' day was a part, were, in fact, very permissive laws. They undoubtedly led to widespread divorce and remarriage and fostered a climate of acceptance, even in Palestine, where Roman law was often rebelled against and/or rejected.

This was surely one primary cause of an important, heated, and popular debate that raged within first-century Judaism, the context out of which Jesus spoke. The debate focused on the intention of the Mosaic law found in Deuteronomy 24:1–4:

> When a man has married a wife, but she does not win his favour because he finds something shameful in her, and he writes her a note of divorce, gives it to her and dismisses her; and suppose after leaving his house she goes off to become the wife of another man, and this next husband turns against her and writes her a note of divorce which he gives her and dismisses her, or dies after making her his wife—then in that case her first husband who dismissed her is not free to take her back to be his wife again after she has become for him unclean. This is abominable to the Lord.

The debate was waged between two prominent rabbinic schools, the schools of Hillel and Shammai. Both agreed that divorce was permitted, largely on the husband's initiative. He could write a certificate, note, or "bill" of divorce which read similar to: "She is not my wife, and I am not her husband" (Hosea 2:2, RSV). By presenting this bill of divorce to his wife, he could send her away (see Isaiah 50:1 and Jeremiah 3:8).

The debate arose, however, over what Moses intended by the phrase "something shameful" in his wife. The more conservative school of Shammai interpreted this to mean that a man could divorce his wife only if she had committed adultery. Hillel's more liberal school of rabbis, on the other hand, took it to mean that a certificate of divorce could be written for anything that displeased the husband, even something as trivial as burning his dinner. Hillel's interpretation, being more liberal, of course grew more popular with the masses, and therefore by the first century divorce and remarriage were nearly as prevalent in Palestine as they were throughout the rest of Rome's Empire.

Living in a situation with such a high incidence of divorce and remarriage and seeing their effects on the lives of countless people, Jesus undoubtedly had some strong feelings concerning these issues. The problem is that he either said very little about them or the early church recorded very little of what he said. Only four statements of Jesus concerning divorce and remarriage are recorded in the Synoptic Gospels. Although somewhat different from one another, most of them are based on a single statement. Moreover, as Theodore Mackin, S.J., points out:

> What these three Synoptic authors give to us are Jesus' words on divorce and remarriage already filtered through the catechetical instruction of different first-generation Christian communities. The significant differences in their several versions of the words are therefore as much ascribable to these early catecheses as they are to the differing editorial intents of the editors themselves. This is enough of a hint . . . of the difficulty we in the twentieth century encounter in trying to recover exactly what Jesus said." (Mackin 1984, pp. 43–44)

We are not the only generation of Christians who have encountered this inability to recover Jesus' actual words. A survey of the history of how the church has addressed the issues of divorce and remarriage will soon show that the church has always had different, and often opposing, views on the subjects. In fact, the cultural context has often shaped the church's teaching. As Peter R. Monkres said: "The church needs to make up its ecclesiastical mind." (Monkres 1985, p. 47). Whether or not the church can "make up its ecclesiastical mind," now or ever, remains to be seen, but given the high incidence of divorce and remarriage in America today, we are certainly being called on to attempt to discern and interpret the words of Jesus for another generation.

Jesus' statements about divorce and remarriage are located only in the Synoptic Gospels: Mark 10:1–12, Matthew 5:31–32, Matthew 19:1–12, and Luke 16:18. The variations in these four statements are interesting to note. Matthew's Jesus appears to side with Rabbi Shammai in the rabbinic debate mentioned above. This would seem logical since Matthew's Gospel is written to an audience made up largely of Jewish Christians familiar with and concerned about rabbinic debates. Mark, however, in chapter 10:1–12 (the oldest and possibly most accurate version), whose Gentile audience would have been more interested in universal moral principles than in Jewish rabbinical debates, quotes Jesus as pointing back beyond Moses to the Creation narratives, quoting Genesis 1:27 and 2:24. Mark's quote, along with Luke's in 16:18, would lead one to believe that Jesus may have viewed the Law of Moses as an excuse for irresponsible behavior or as an accommodation to our sinful human nature. Many of his other conversations with the Pharisees would confirm this notion also. Therefore, rather than accommodating and entering into the debate of the Pharisees, Jesus is concerning himself, as he so often does, not with the "letter of the law," but with the spirit of the law, the intention with which the law was given, the intention of God. In so doing, Jesus makes it perfectly clear that divorce and remarriage are not what God intended.

God's intention is made clear in Genesis 2:18–25. While the animals do not have a nature that corresponds to that of the man, and thus are not "fit" (RSV) companions, the woman is referred to as "bone from my bones, flesh from my flesh" (v. 23). She is, therefore, equally human to the man. "That is why a man leaves his father and mother and is united to his wife, and the two become one flesh" (v. 24). The two complement each other, fulfill each other's needs, and make up for each other's deficiencies. In short, they offer wholeness to each other. Their union is, therefore, God-willed, God-intended, an integral dimension of God's plan for creation.

The writings of Paul go on to affirm this message as well. In I Corinthians 7:10–11, one of Paul's very rare direct references to specific teachings of Jesus, we read these words: "To the married I give this ruling, which is not mine but the Lord's: a wife must not separate herself from her husband; if she does, she must either remain unmarried or be reconciled to her husband; and the husband must not divorce his wife." In interpreting these words, one must remember that what is written in chapter seven of First Corinthians is in response to a direct question. The question, which seems to have had more to do with sex than with marriage, wonders whether marriage is still a legitimate option for Christian people.

Given Paul's expectation of the imminent return of Christ, he felt that his readers needed to devote all their attention to the Lord, a task that is far easier for those who do not have all the earthly concerns that a spouse and family necessarily evoke. But if one is already married, one should remain married, because Jesus does not condone divorce.

On the other hand, in spite of Jesus' statements about divorce and remarriage, Paul presumes that divorces will occur, some precisely because a spouse becomes a Christian. In fact, in verse 15 of the same chapter, he makes a very clear and important pastoral statement that those Christians who are not able to live "in peace" with their non-Christian spouses are no longer bound to honor their marriage covenant and are free to divorce. (The church later termed this the "Pauline Privilege," which the Roman Catholic Church still uses today to justify annulments.) Victor Paul Furnish offers a helpful interpretation of verse 15:

> He would appear to be unwilling to sanction the idea that marriage is an end in and of itself that must be maintained at any cost. Here Paul shows a sensitivity to the importance of the quality of a marriage relationship for which he is seldom given credit. When, practically, the relationship between a husband and wife is no longer characterized by mutual respect, love, and faithfulness, then separation is permissible. (Furnish 1979, pp. 45–46)

Paul's "sensitivity" in verse 15, combined with the lack of "credit" he usually receives for it, makes an important point, a point summed up very powerfully by James M. Efird:

> It is an interesting phenomenon to see passages taken from Jesus' teaching and Paul's letters used in . . . an absolute and legalistic manner. That is a curious situation. For here were two persons who were above all else opposed to legalism, but some have made their teachings into a new legalism. . . . It is also an interesting point that even though Paul knew Jesus' teaching about marriage and divorce, he did not interpret it literally or legalistically! The process of making a legalism of such sayings came later than Paul. (Efird 1985, pp. 87–88)

The point is that on the one hand this "legalism" has correctly upheld the church's understanding that marriage is a gift, ordained by God, for the health, happiness, well-being, and wholeness of human beings, and therefore that divorce and remarriage are not part of God's intention. On the other hand, in so doing, it has too often denied another equally important dimension of the gospel, which is just as integral to the church's theology, and that is forgiveness, sometimes called "the gospel of grace."

The "gospel of grace" often tends to be more evident in Jesus' actions than in his teachings. Therefore, it is important to examine his teachings in light of the rest of the gospel. In so doing, we find that even though Jesus firmly upholds the standards, the will, the intention of God in his teachings, such as the Sermon on the Mount discourses, in practice he forgives a woman "caught in the act of adultery" (John 7:53—8:11, RSV); he affirms the personhood of the despised tax collector, Zacchaeus, by inviting himself to dine in Zacchaeus' home (Luke 19:1–10); and he breaks down traditional cultural barriers in order to speak with and offer "life" to a Samaritan woman who had five husbands and is living out of wedlock with a sixth man (John 4:5–30). These stories, and many more, reveal that Jesus did not see himself as a lawgiver, in spite of the Pharisees' many attempts to make him one. In such encounters with people, Jesus is never judgmental or punishing, but understanding, affirming, and forgiving, thereby offering people opportunities to change their lives. He is always life-promoting, as opposed to being life-denying, which the Pharisees often are. Therefore, it would be presumptuous to argue that his divorce-and-remarriage statements, the Beatitudes, and other such teachings are meant to be "Christian laws."

Indeed, these teachings might be better interpreted as Jesus' way of shocking his listeners into examining their own behavior, a popular teaching technique among ancient rabbis. Rather than intending his teachings to be understood and upheld legalistically, Jesus provided them as moral principles by which people in his audience were to compare their own behavior, and toward which they were to strive.

One might further assert that difficult teachings such as these might be meant by Jesus to make an important statement to the self-righteous Pharisees. If they desired to be declared righteous on the basis of their keeping of the law, then they should understand how "high" the law really is. As Jesus said, "Do not suppose that I have come to abolish the Law and the prophets; I did not come to abolish, but to complete" (Matt. 5:17). The law encompasses far more than the Mosaic law; indeed, it encompasses the very will, purpose, and intention of God. So you must "be perfect, as your [God] is perfect" (Matt. 5:48, RSV). Quite obviously neither the Pharisees nor anyone else can "measure up" to the standards of God. Even the proud and self-righteous are humbled beside such ideals as these.

Therefore, the case can be argued that Jesus never meant to have these high standards, these intentions of God, interpreted as laws. Rather, he meant to uphold them as the ideal, the vision toward which we are to strive and against which we can measure our growth. In the process of doing this, we cannot help realizing just how guilty and helpless we really are, even "the best of us." Only with such a realization can we turn to God in a spirit of faith and trust, realizing and admitting our dependence on the grace and love of our divine sustainer. As Martin Luther finally realized, we find righteousness not by living up to these high standards, but by our faith in God.

As usual, then, Jesus is life-promoting and -freeing. Rather than giving us a law that will imprison us, Jesus is providing a standard or ideal that will challenge us to faithfulness and righteousness, and thereby draw us closer to God and neighbor. As such, he offers us a gift of grace in what at first appears to be a harsh and firm law.

It would have been out of character, however, for Jesus to deny the destructive reality of human sin and its toll on many marriages. Unfortunately, many marriages are life-denying rather than life-promoting for one or both spouses, and often for the children as well. While God's will and purpose are perfect, human beings are not. Therefore, Jesus would not deny that marriage covenants can, will, and sometimes should be broken. When we do break them, however, we must evaluate ourselves by these high standards of righteousness, just as we must when we pass judgment on a neighbor or seek revenge against someone who has wronged us. Beside these high intentions of God, our sin, or separation (distance) from God, spouse, and others, is exposed if we have eyes to see it. But, as long as pride and self-righteousness blind us we will not see it, and in that case God cannot help us. When we do see it, however, Jesus invites us to know our need of God, to admit our brokenness, and to trust God to forgive and renew us. When we do that, as he has taught us by his teachings as well as by his very life, then the redeeming power of God, which transformed the agony of the cross into the joy of Easter, will be at work in our lives, offering us newness of life as well. In this regard, Eduard Schweizer, in his commentary *The Good News According to Mark*, states that "Divorce *can* be a sign of repentance by which two people face up to their failure. It *can* be a confession that they have not succeeded in living according to God's will, i.e., on the basis of his gift. Divorce *can*, therefore, set one free to experience anew the mercy of God" (Schweizer 1970, p. 205). That mercy is portrayed in the Gospels in the person of Jesus as he provides healing, forgiveness, love, and grace to all who know their need of God, even the "worst" of sinners.

In cases of divorce and remarriage, the church has an opportunity to imitate the life-giving ministry of Jesus, and to be an arm or an instrument of God's mercy, love, and redemption. This does not mean that we should cease proclaiming the high standards and intention of God, any more than Jesus did. It does mean, however, that we must recognize the painful reality of divorce and work to transform its pain and guilt into new life for the individuals and families involved. For many, that new life will come as they experience a positive, healthy, and enduring remarriage.

If the church is to fulfill its call to be the body of Christ, carrying on his words and deeds and continuing his ministry, can we condemn remarriage? Is that not ignoring "the gospel of grace"? Is that not denying the primary truth on which the church is built: that our God is a redeeming God, always at work, transforming crucifixions of every kind into resurrections to new life?

The fact is that there is only one faithful response to the question about remarriage in the church following divorce. That response is the one we see in the compassionate, forgiving, loving Jesus, interacting with people throughout the Gospels, bringing healing, hope, and new life to all. That response is the one we see in a church that reaches out in love to adults and children who are about to become a stepfamily, takes them seriously, and helps them prepare for the unique joys, struggles, and challenges that lie ahead.

CHAPTER THREE

Preparing Families
for Remarriage in the Church:
A Model Process

Frank and Helen are in their late fifties, and each has three grown children. Frank is a widower and Helen has been divorced. Because of Helen's strong Roman Catholic background, she began the remarriage preparation process feeling very guilty and defensive about her divorce and remarriage. Early in the second session the minister, who knew Frank very well from his active involvement in the church and from ministry with his first wife during her long bout with cancer, led the couple in a Bible study on the divorce and remarriage texts. As the study progressed, the look of relief on Helen's face became obvious. She described having a load lifted from her shoulders. Since that time, she has not only felt extremely comfortable and confident about her marriage to Frank, but she has also become a much happier and more outgoing person. She and Frank have even had training for, and are now leading, an ongoing support group in the church for separated, divorced, and widowed people. She has, indeed, taken seriously this charge that she chose to have included in her remarriage ceremony:

Helen, as you contemplate the meaning and importance of marriage, and the vows that you are about to make to Frank, I am sure that you are deeply aware of your first marriage. That marriage failed, and, with it, all your goals and aspirations for that union. Today, I charge you to let go of that old relationship, and to dedicate yourself, wholly and completely, to this new relationship. Remember, as Christians, we affirm that it is God who gives you to each other and offers you this new opportunity to develop a meaningful and lasting marriage relationship. We are an Easter people, and remarriage can be seen as a symbol of resurrection and new life. As Jesus came forth from the tomb of death into a new life, so, out of the ashes of your former marriage, you are offered new life this day. Therefore, give yourself fully to Frank, in both the good and difficult times ahead, and you will know the renewal of life that God offers you this day.

The journey that Frank and Helen have taken has been remarkable. People who have known them for the duration of their journey together often remark about the transformation they have witnessed. Frank and Helen are quick to tell them that "it was the healing, forgiving love of Christ, which we experienced as we prepared for our remarriage and on our wedding day, that has changed our lives." In the case of Helen and Frank, therefore, the primary goal of the remarriage preparation process was accomplished.

A second goal of the process is to provide one of the earliest and most meaningful opportunities for the new stepfamily to develop a sense of connection and unity. Two of the most important factors in any family's strength and adaptability are the shared history and the common rituals and traditions among its members. Shared history includes two elements. First, it is common memory of events that the family members have experienced together, such as Disney World vacations and concerts by favorite musicians. In addition, it is the everyday events that the family has shared, such as breakfast on the deck and friendly arguments over whose turn it is for the bathroom. Common rituals and traditions are the normal patterns that a particular family has chosen for doing certain tasks, spending certain holidays and the like. For example, some families clean the house together every Saturday morning; others spend every Thanksgiving Day morning at the football game. Some spend every Sunday morning in church before going to Grandma's for lunch; others decide what to do each weekend at a family meeting every Thursday night. Members of stepfamilies, on the other hand, come into the new family unit with different histories, values, and traditions, with very little to bind them together and strengthen them as a unit. In fact, rituals and traditions they have grown up with and cherished often clash with those of their new stepparent and stepsiblings. The remarriage preparation process, therefore, has as a goal offering them a foundation stone on which they can begin to build and unify. In order to accomplish this goal, a basic ingredient of this preparation process is its inclusion of all immediate family members: parents, stepparents, and children and stepchildren, both custodial and noncustodial, ages four to seventeen. Occasionally older children and other significant extended-family members are also included, depending on the circumstances of a given family situation. Together they share the counseling process which culminates in creating and participating in their own specially designed ceremony of remarriage.

In developing a process for preparing couples and their families for remarriage, one must consider many issues and implications. Among them are the unique dynamics, both positive and negative, that are normally operative in stepfamilies; the prevalent myths regarding stepfamily living; the individual needs of family members in some cases; the qualities and characteristics of functioning and fulfilled stepfamilies, and how to assist any given family in developing them; the time, educational and financial requirements, and limitations of the pastor and/or other counselors as well as of the family itself; the support or lack of support received from the local church community as well as the wider church; the necessity to refer some families to counselors with specialized experience or qualifications; and more. All these issues have been considered in the development of this process and will be explored further as the process is outlined.

The remarriage preparation process normally requires four counseling sessions prior to the wedding rehearsal and the wedding itself, depending on the needs of the individual families. More can be added, if necessary, with all, some, or one of the members. Only the first session does not include all family members. This is because it is the initial, introductory interview, often many months before the wedding, when the pastor and the couple meet for both to contemplate whether to go farther with the process. It is designed to take approximately one to one and one-half hours.

The second and third sessions tend to be longer if the pastor or counselor works with both the adults and the children, because separate time is required for each during these sessions. An alternative that has been used successfully is to have a separate counselor do some of the work with the children.

The children's counselor must be a compassionate and well-trained layperson chosen to assist the minister. He or she must have experience (if possible, professional experience) working with children and also be comfortable with adults. While it is not necessary for the counselor to have experienced divorce and remarriage, it may be helpful. Training and/or study in the effects of divorce and remarriage on children is essential. Further training in the dynamics of this preparation process is also important. Beyond that, other significant qualities of this children's counselor are a sensitivity to youngsters' needs and fears; an ability to see this work as a ministry of love; a flexibility about the time commitment involved in this work; and an ability to communicate the needs, hopes, fears, and feelings of the children to the minister, who can use this knowledge, without breaking confidence, in working with the couple. The children's counselor must also be able to think reflectively and deeply about verbal and nonverbal cues, family dynamics, hidden agendas, and the like.

The training of the children's counselor(s) is twofold. First, an understanding of the effects of divorce and remarriage on children at various ages, as well as their feelings about those effects, must be developed. As with ministers using this process, some of that knowledge can be obtained from this book. In addition, that person can and should study some of the literature on the subject that is mentioned in "Suggestions for Further Study." Second, the minister needs to go over the preparation process thoroughly with the counselor, highlighting its goals and objectives and explaining its structure.

The fourth session in the process is significantly shorter, usually less than one hour. At this time, the ceremony is developed into its final form, based on homework the family has done together prior to the session.

Homework between sessions is an integral part of the entire process for both the adults and the children, sometimes requiring them to work together. Although the content of all the sessions will be discussed in more detail in the chapters that follow, a brief overview of each is provided here.

The first session is often the pastor's and the couple's first opportunity to meet one another. Here the minister hears each one's story as well as the story of their courtship, and tries to discern the strengths and the needs of their relationship. They discuss their feelings about their previous marriage(s) and spouse(s) and what effects they feel divorce has had on both themselves and their children. They are asked about their family structure in the past and present, as well as their hopes for it in the future. Their experiences in the church regarding their divorce(s) and their decision to remarry, as well as their feelings about those experiences, are examined. The support they have received and not received, and from whom, is an important topic of discussion, as is their reason for desiring Christian marriage and their attraction to this particular church.

Throughout this first session, the minister assesses this couple's relationship and readiness for remarriage, the impact of the past marriage(s) on this one, and what feelings, issues, fears, and illusions might need to be addressed in future counseling sessions. Also assessed are the needs of the children, as well as the family's willingness to commit themselves to the church's remarriage preparation process after the minister has detailed it to them. If, following this session, both the pastor and the couple feel positive about continuing the process, a date is agreed on for session two. This may be months away, since the second and following sessions should be held no more than three months prior to the wedding date.

In preparation for the second session, the couple are requested to make separate lists of what they *want*, *need*, and *feel* regarding their new marriage. They are not to share these lists until that session.

All the couple's children, both custodial and noncustodial, from the ages of four through seventeen, are invited to the second session. In some cases it may not be possible for some or all to attend, but all are invited. Those under age four are usually too young to remember their parents' divorce or to participate meaningfully in the counseling process. Those over seventeen should, of course, be considered and have the opportunity to meet with the pastor. They are, however, too mature for the counseling process developed here, and often no longer integrally involved in their parent's home or family. If a children's counselor is being used, that person should be briefed and invited to attend also.

Session two begins the more intensive work in preparation for remarriage. After beginning with an informal time of sharing general conversation in order to help ease any tension, the pastor explains to the children their importance to the couple and to the new family that will be created by their marriage. That is why they are being given their own chance to prepare for it, just as the couple are. This not only publicly affirms the place of the children in the new family, but also helps all of them think of themselves as a family unit. As the minister explains how the preparation process works, highlighting that part in which they will create their own unique wedding ceremony, it is noted that the purpose of the process is to help them learn about the blessings and the struggles that stepfamilies usually have, how to communicate better with one another, and ways that each one can help the family become stronger, healthier, and happier.

After this introductory period, the children either remain with the minister while the parents are excused for thirty to sixty minutes, or remain with the children's counselor while their parents go with the minister to a separate room. As outlined in chapter 7, the children are then led in exploring their feelings with regard to the divorce of their biological parents. The tool for this process, a children's workbook entitled "My Parent Is Getting Remarried," is printed at the end of this book. Clergy and counselors may reproduce it as needed. Then the homework for the next session is introduced. At present the best and most useful and complete resource for children on the issue of remarriage and stepfamilies is Helen Coale

Lewis' book *All About Families the Second Time Around*. I give it to the children as a gift and ask that they read it, together with their parent and almost-stepparent, discussing it and completing the worksheets in it before the next session. They may also wish to share it with their other biological parent. Copies of the book may be obtained separately or in bulk from:

Helen Coale Lewis
c/o Atlanta Area Child Guidance Clinic
2531 Briarcliff Road, N.E. Suite 215
Atlanta, GA 30329   (404) 636-5875

If the minister is the one who will be with the children, prior arrangements should have been made for their care during their parent's session. In some cases, children are old enough to care for themselves or each other. In other cases, a babysitter or relative might be available or a volunteer in the church might be called on.

The adults also begin their session by focusing on their divorce(s): the reasons for it; their feelings about it, as well as about the former spouse; their responsibility in the breakdown of the previous marriage(s); how they have changed or not as a result; and why they feel that this new marriage will be stronger. Depending on the couple, this discussion may be lengthy or brief. The minister works toward clarifying and absolving guilt, recognizing patterns of behavior that may affect the new marriage, and resolving feelings about the past that could be problematic in the future. It is often helpful at this point to include a brief Bible study, using some of the material presented in chapter 2. For some couples, it may even be appropriate to provide some printed Bible-study materials for further consideration at home.

After looking at their pasts, the couple are then led in an examination of their present relationship, primarily in regard to communication, parenting, stepparenting, and conflict resolution. Then, using their homework lists as a basis for discussion, the couple are asked to discuss their expectations of each other and of the marriage. Finally, as time permits, their future goals in regard to parenting and stepparenting styles, roles, and responsibilities are shared and negotiated.

In preparation for session three, the couple are given the discussion sheet, explained in chapter 5, entitled "Love and Marriage." This sheet is to be done as homework. Additional homework will include working on the children's new book with them; listening to Elizabeth Einstein's audiotapes, *The Stepfamily Journey* (1987) and *Stepfamily Living: Myths and Realities* (1985), which may be obtained from E. Einstein Enterprises c/o Elizabeth Einstein, P.O. Box 6760, Ithaca, New York, 14851; and considering their relationship in the light of a statement about wholeness that the minister will share with them. Session two ends with a gathering of the entire family for brief sharing and conversation, along with a closing prayer.

The third session, like the second, begins and ends with a brief, informal gathering time for all who are part of the process. During the opening time, general comments are solicited about their work in Helen Coale Lewis' book. The children then continue to work with the minister or children's counselor, as outlined more fully in chapter 7. This time they focus on the remarriage of their parent, examining the issues in stepfamily living that are addressed in Lewis' book, that is, titles, names, feelings, the role of the stepparent, family history, the sharing of self and learning about others, "games" that stepfamilies often play, the myth of "instant love," loyalty conflicts, and creating new "special event days." Then they discuss some helpful ways for the children to handle the upcoming events and evaluate their learnings from the sessions. The counselor or minister must be prepared, of course, in either session two or session three, to abandon the agenda in order to discuss any major issue that might arise.

As described in chapter 6, session three for the adults continues with any unresolved issues from session two, or other issues that the pastor raises based on the session with the children or discussion with the children's counselor. The couple are then asked to share their thoughts and reflections about the tapes, as well as about the idea of "wholeness" as the pastor described it in session two. Finally, the major task of the session is to utilize the couple's "Love and Marriage" homework, as chapter 6 elaborates, to help them set goals and develop priorities for their relationship as well as create a faithful and life-giving vision of what their marriage and stepfamily can become, incorporating as many dimensions of healthy, balanced marital and family relationships as possible. As time permits, any other unresolved issues and concerns may be shared and discussed.

Session three is closed with a gathering of the entire new family for sharing, conversation, and prayer. Before closing, however, the minister assigns their homework for session four, to work together using liturgical materials provided by the minister to create an appropriate and unique wedding ceremony.

If a children's counselor has been used, that person's work is usually finished after session three. However, if the children were unable to complete their work in sessions two and three, session four may be used as a time for them to finish, either with the counselor or with the minister. The same is true for the adults, who may use the beginning of session four to resolve any "old business" before working with the minister on the preparation of their ceremony. If there are no other issues to discuss, the family can remain together and work on the ceremony with the minister.

As described in chapter 8, the minister goes over with the family each of their choices for the various parts of the ceremony, reading each one aloud to make sure that the service "flows" and says what the family wishes. The family's reasons for making the choices they made are then discussed. When the service has been developed to everyone's satisfaction, other questions pertaining to the details of the service, such as the wedding party, the rehearsal, the decorating of the church, pictures, and the like, can be raised. Other comments and reflections are then shared, along with a statement by the pastor about "coming back anytime" should any or all of them need to talk about issues, concerns, or problems after the wedding. Hands are then joined and a prayer offered to conclude the fourth session. Normally the family does not meet with the pastor again until the rehearsal and then the wedding itself.

The chapters that follow will further detail this process. In them, the agenda for each session will be examined more fully, along with the theory behind using that agenda. That theory might be best summarized, however, in this statement by Elizabeth Einstein and

Linda Albert in their book *Stepfamily Living: Preparing for Remarriage:*

> A loving and successful stepfamily depends upon how well adults prepare themselves and their children for remarriage. The getting ready time of courtship becomes far more complex than the first time around. . . .
>
> Within the first three to five years of stepfamily living, more remarriages end in divorce than first marriages. This sad statistic, in part representing inadequate remarriage preparation, reflects a dangerous duo: poor resolution of former relationships and a lack of information about what living in a stepfamily will be like. (Einstein and Albert 1983, pp. 3–4)

CHAPTER FOUR

Session 1:
Building the Foundation

It can be argued that the initial session in remarriage preparation is the most important in the entire process in that the first meeting sets the tone, or builds the foundation upon which the entire process rests. Because the process is brief and hopes to accomplish much, couples and their families must take it seriously and move very quickly to a deep and intimate level of openness and sharing. To foster this, a minister or counselor may use two important techniques. First, respond to all initial inquiries about weddings in a businesslike, noncommittal fashion: "The wedding date you desire is open, and I would be happy to pencil you in tentatively. However, I never consent to perform a wedding until I have met the couple, discussed their relationship and plans with them, and decided that this marriage is something I can feel positive about, and in good conscience officiate at. If you would like to schedule an initial session with me as soon as possible, I will give you a firm answer following it."

This technique is important for two reasons. First, it brings out whether the couple are confident enough in the quality and strength of their relationship to expose it to the possibility of a negative response. Second, it makes them nervous and puts them on edge, so that they begin to explore for themselves some of the possible reasons why their marriage could be refused. While this can remove some of the "stars in their eyes," it can also make them over-defensive about their relationship. The minister or counselor needs to look carefully for and question what appears to be overdefensive behavior.

The second technique to help couples take the process seriously and move quickly to a deep level of sharing is the use of questions in the first session that catch them off guard and force them to think deeply about themselves and their relationship. For example, after some initial, get-acquainted conversation, I always begin session one by asking, "Why do you want to get married? Why not just live together?" Hardly an expected question from a minister, it surprises couples and usually exposes how committed each partner is to the covenant of marriage, so that we can discuss it in more detail. Fears, values, and areas of conflict often begin to surface. The second question continues to probe: "Why do you wish to be married in a church? Why not just go to a justice of the peace?" This question raises the issue of faith immediately. Again differences of opinion tend to surface quickly, as do their feelings about the church. In cases where one or both partners have experienced divorce, it is important to examine what messages they have received from the church, any guilt that may be unresolved, and their sense of their own relationship with God. Occasionally, this may result in a referral to a justice of the peace if they seek "a pretty place" rather than Christian marriage.

The third question is: "How did you decide to come to this church for your wedding?" Unless both partners are members of the church, this is a valid and important question. If one is a member, it is important to know the couple's thought process in arriving at this decision. If neither is a member, it is important to know who referred them, or how they found the church. Often, it is second choice to their own church, which refuses to marry them because of the divorce of one or both. In such cases, it is important to examine their feelings about that rejection, and its implications concerning their relationship with God. In so doing, one can discover their needs in relation to studying and interpreting the Scriptures, specifically those parts concerned with divorce and remarriage, hearing a message of absolution from this church or their own, and exploring their own faith journeys. Conceivably, this process could lead the minister to suggest that they apply for annulment(s) in order to be married in their own church. Or, depending on the couple, it may also lead into an immediate discussion of the biblical materials regarding divorce and remarriage, providing Bible-study literature for reading and discussion at home, or placing a Bible study item on the agenda for the second session.

These and other difficult questions provide an important beginning to the preparation process because they encourage honesty and intimacy as well as exposing fears, value differences, and potential areas of conflict. The minister or counselor must be careful as these questions are discussed to appear nonjudgmental and impartial. This is the beginning of the pastoral relationship with these couples. If they are to experience God's love, forgiveness, and renewal, the primary goal of the process, they must first feel these from their pastor.

Trish and Mike wrote, following their remarriage:

> When I first called inquiring about you performing ceremonies, you sounded very businesslike. I was a little anxious about meeting with you. Meeting and talking with you in person changed that feeling. You were very sincere and caring, I felt. Mike says in no way did he feel judged.

Tom and Sarah, the couple mentioned in chapter 1, also wrote about the experience:

> I remember the first time we met you. You didn't say you'd marry us right away. You had to talk to us first. As we talked you brought out all the anger, hurt, and frustration we had felt for so long since our divorces. That session clearly showed us that our divorces were a handicap, not a stigma. You simply wanted us to exorcise old ghosts, learn from the misery of our past, and make our relationship more honest and secure. You didn't judge us—you made us see that we should stop judging ourselves. When you said you'd marry us, we were very happy because we felt a friend would be sharing that special moment with us.

As Tom and Sarah suggest, after the initial questions the first session is used to explore the couple's own relationship, as well as the significant events in each one's past that helped make them who they are and brought them to this time and place.

Questions might continue as follows: "Tell me about how you met, and where, and how long ago? What has your relationship been like since then? Would you share with me some of the highlights of your relationship, both ups and downs?" These questions elicit basic data concerning the growth of their relationship, the extent of their courtship, and any serious conflict areas that have arisen. If there have been serious conflicts or major breakups during their courtship, further discussion will be necessary.

After looking briefly at the present relationship, it is important to discuss the divorce of either or both partners, as the case may be. "How long have you been divorced?" If the couple knew each other, or dated, prior to the divorce of one or both, it should be discussed, especially with regard to any guilt that may be unresolved. "And what happened to that relationship?" Here the minister must be very sensitive to nonverbal communication, tone of voice, and phrasing. Very often unresolved feelings of guilt, anger, pain, denial, inadequacy, hatred, and fear are transmitted. These must be explored and dealt with sensitively during the next one or two sessions. Occasionally it may be beneficial to meet privately with one or both partners in order most effectively to work through and resolve these feelings. In almost all cases an assurance of forgiveness must be offered and heard before healing can occur. This might be done through Bible study, as with Frank and Helen in chapter 3, or liturgically, as we shall see in chapter 8.

"What kind of response, if any, did you get from your church as you were divorcing, or after it?" is another important question that provides an additional opportunity to explore each person's feelings about the church. If those feelings are negative, the minister has an opportunity to try to transform those feelings to positive ones, and perhaps to help build a stronger relationship with the church.

"What kind of response did you receive from your family and friends during your divorce, and since then?" introduces the issue of extended family and friends. It also examines where the couple's support systems are and are not located, and often reveals any unresolved guilt, tension, fear, anger, hatred, and denial.

While it is essential to examine the divorce(s) and the couple's feelings about this, it is just as important not to end the first session in the past. More can and will be dealt with later in regard to the divorce(s). Therefore, the issue of family and friends is usually an appropriate bridge back to the present: "How do your family and friends feel about your present relationship, and your upcoming marriage?" Often in-law problems and fears, as well as other areas of conflict, surface here. Usually discussion can result in compromises that are acceptable to both partners.

The issue of children also needs to be raised at this first session: "Does either one of you have children from your previous marriage?" If so, then, "What are their names and ages? What are their living arrangements? Do they live with you or visit you? How do you each feel about that arrangement?" Usually these questions and the ones that follow generate a multitude of feelings in both partners: guilt, anger, jealousy, remorse, sadness, disappointment, resentment, confusion, fear, inadequacy. These feelings will be dealt with throughout the preparation process and after. Having the children involved in the process, and included in the ceremony, usually proves very helpful in resolving many of these feelings. Occasionally, sometime during the process, it may be appropriate to discuss the adoption of the child(ren) by the new stepparent, which also may be of help in the resolution of some of these feelings. Adoption rarely provides such help, however. Therefore, if it is of interest to parent and stepparent, before any such plans are made, or mention of it made to a child, it should be thoroughly discussed with someone with expertise in the area of adoption and its impact on children and families. In most cases, this will require a referral that has been well researched by the pastor.

"Do you have to pay child support or alimony payments? Are you going to be able to continue those after you get remarried? How do you feel about having to make them?" These questions address several important issues: the couple's financial situation, obligations, and ability; their sense of responsibility to take the consequences of choices made (how they handle past and present responsibilities can be a good indicator of how they will handle future ones); and unity or conflict over each one's obligation for past decisions.

"How old were the children as the divorce was happening? What kind of effect do you think it had on them?" Of course, this question cannot be dealt with fully or adequately in this first session, but it is important to start considering it.

"How do the children feel about the idea of having a new stepparent? How do you get along with them?" It is often helpful to remind the stepparent that she or he is not just marrying a spouse, but a family, and that how the children feel is very important to the well-being of the marriage itself. The minister needs to be sensitive to the level of bonding that has taken place and to encourage the stepparent to consciously watch for opportunities to develop stronger bonds. This must be done carefully, however, so as not to increase any confusion or conflict in the children about loyalties and boundaries. The stepparent is not, in most cases, trying to replace a biological parent, to be another mom or dad.

Finally, it is helpful in the first session to discuss the couple's families of origin: "Tell me about your families of origin. Where were you in the birth order? What was it like growing up in your family? How did your parents interact? Has anyone in your family ever been divorced or remarried? How did that make you feel? What do you remember as the major joys and struggles of growing up?" These questions are very important to consider in attempting to discover the strengths and potential weaknesses in the couple's relationship. The minister can deduce from the answers the implications of each partner's birth order, possible dependency needs, the values that each learned and how each one's coincides with the other's, the strength and stability (or lack of it) of the models they had for marriage relationships, and like matters. Often information and feelings come out that can be dealt with more thoroughly in future sessions.

By the time a minister or counselor has explored all these areas and issues with the couple, that person will have a good sense of the strengths and areas of need in their relationship. In addition, a great deal of data will have been gathered and, after the couple leaves, recorded for use in later sessions. With all this information in mind, the minister or counselor needs to make an immediate decision about officiating at the couple's wedding. Normally, this is not difficult, but it is important to share with the couple the reasoning behind a positive or negative decision. When the answer is negative or tentative, suggestions should be made about steps they can take to work on the area(s) that either prevent the minister from officiating or make the minister uncomfortable. For example, it may be in the couple's best interest to go through the process of receiving an annulment from their own church, even though they had hoped to avoid the time and expense of it. In other cases, there may be an issue in their relationship that needs expertise and qualifications beyond that of the minister. In this case, the minister should suggest a referral, even if it means researching who an appropriate person would be for such a referral. If a referral is made and accepted, the wedding date may need only to be postponed or the counseling done simultaneously with their marriage preparation. Making the referral in a caring way and maintaining close contact with the couple during their counseling may make the experience very positive and life-giving.

Ted and Pat, for example, a couple in their forties, were both church members. Ted had been both divorced and widowed, and Pat was divorced. Knowing and caring for both, I enjoyed watching their relationship grow and take shape over several years. As we began preparing for their marriage, I was surprised when Pat shared some fears that she had about Ted's sexual orientation. She had reason to think he might be an active bisexual. While I had trouble believing it, I wanted to be sure that her feelings were resolved before proceeding. That meant that a referral was necessary. In spite of his shock and anger at Pat's suggestion, Ted agreed to go with Pat to see a certified sex therapist, who would help them work through this issue. I maintained regular contact with each during this period, and was ready to continue preparing for their wedding whenever they were ready. Though they suffered the embarrassment of postponing their well-publicized wedding date, the marriage they finally entered was more honest, trusting, and satisfying than either of them had ever experienced or hoped for. Pat writes: "Thank you for being gentle and caring. I dared to be honest even though I knew it would hurt Ted.

The therapist was good, but it was difficult, and we were both scared. We hated to postpone our wedding, but sure glad we did. Thank you, Gordon."

It is not only the minister or counselor who finds this first session important for studying the strengths, needs, and dynamics of a couple's relationship. The couple does as well. David and Wendy wrote about their first session: "Although both of us were nervous about confronting our problem areas, and sometimes surprised by each other's thoughts, we feel that the initial session was very helpful. You handled the session in such a loving, positive way."

Sometimes the couple realizes that there is a problem, even after the minister or counselor has said yes to performing the ceremony. It was shortly after session one when I received a call from Donna, informing me that she and Peter had decided to postpone their wedding. She said: "Our session with you made us realize that we are not ready for marriage. We have too many differences to work out. We didn't know how many things we have to consider, and I sure would hate to put Sarah (her twelve-year-old daughter) through another divorce." It was not long after that call that Sarah told me at youth fellowship that her mom and Peter were no longer seeing each other.

The first session is important to both the minister and the couple. It builds the important foundation of trust, honesty, and deep sharing that the entire process requires. It also helps the pastor and the couple see the gifts and the challenges of the relationship, and provides many topics for future discussions. It enables the couple to acknowledge and negotiate issues of conflict and tension. It allows referrals to be made when necessary, before the wedding date has been confirmed by the minister and the church, and even gives the minister an opportunity to refuse a wedding that gives rise to a strong level of discomfort.

At the conclusion of this session, once the minister or counselor has decided to continue the process with a couple, the couple need to be well informed about the rest of the process, especially the work that will be done with the children. They may decide that it is too much for them to go through, or not appropriate for their family. While this response is rare, it has happened. Therefore, the minister or counselor needs to think about a response to such a decision.

Concerns with regard to the children are often the stumbling block. While I refuse to officiate at a remarriage unless I have had a chance to do at least some work with the children, I will occasionally vary the process to meet the needs of certain families. Some want a separate children's counselor; others do not. Some desire or need a separate session hour for the children; others ask me to try to do all my work with the children in one session, even if it is an extended one. Often there are custody and/or visitation arrangements that necessitate such changes, and I vary the process to accommodate their needs. Working with stepfamilies generally requires some flexibility simply because of the complexity of these families and their lifestyles.

Once the process has been agreed on, the homework is assigned. In preparation for the second session, the couple are requested to make separate lists which they are not to share until that session. On the lists, they are to include: (1) what they *want* from their partner and from their marriage; (2) what they *need* from their partner and from their marriage; (3) how they *feel* about their partner and their marriage. These will offer the couple and minister an opportunity in session two to clarify expectations and explore any "hidden agendas."

While this is an important task for any couple entering marriage, it is extremely important for those preparing to remarry, because so often each one will need to give up roles, functions, and boundaries that were operative in their previous relationship as well as negotiating and clarifying their new ones. A date for the next session is then chosen.

When the couple has departed, data from the first session that might prove helpful in future sessions can be recorded and filed. If a children's counselor will be used, appropriate information and data can be passed on to assist that person in any planning or research that might need to be done before meeting with the children.

CHAPTER FIVE

Session 2:
Looking at Yesterday
and Today with the Couple

Seeing six people walk into the office—two adults, each with two children under twelve—to prepare for a wedding only three months away, can intimidate a minister. Moreover, only two of those children, the woman's two, will live in the new household created by this marriage. The other two will "visit" every other weekend and one night each week. "Where do I begin?" one might ask.

Session two often opens with such a situation. That is the reason for beginning with light conversation, as described in chapter 3. It is a time to get a sense of how each one is feeling about this appointment, and probably about the wedding itself. The minister or counselor will need to converse directly with each one during this time, looking for signs of anger, jealousy, distrust and depression, or nervous giggling. Rivalries between children, a stepparent's discomfort with children, a child's extreme insecurity, a parent's confusion about dealing with children, and many other concerns that need to be worked through later, are likely to be observed by an aware pastor (and children's counselor if one is being used). It is also a time to begin building trust with the family, as connections are made with each member in a supportive, nonthreatening, nonjudgmental atmosphere. The hope is that they will begin to trust the staff and the process as it is described to them, so that they can relax and share more and more of their thoughts and feelings during this session and the next.

Usually, before the end of this initial phase of session two, the minister and children's counselor have assessed at least some of this family's gifts and problem areas. Knowing these, and therefore having some goals in mind, they begin to relax as well. Then it is usually time to separate the couple and children and begin the more intensive work of session two. As indicated in chapter 3, the minister can offer back-to-back sessions, one with the children and the other with the couple, or a children's counselor may work with the children while the pastor works with the couple.

Chapter 7 will outline the work to be done with the children; this chapter will concentrate on the couple. In both cases, the session is designed to help the family members look back at the past, to explore their feelings about the divorce and life since the divorce and begin resolving these feelings as much as possible, and to assist the family members in attaining an emotional divorce from their previous family so that they can invest themselves in this new one. The session, for both the couple and the children, is also a beginning in discovering their feelings, hopes, concerns, fears, and joys regarding this marriage and the family that will result from it.

With the data gathered during the first session, the minister can begin the second session with a list of areas that need further exploration, discussion, compromising, or resolving. The discussion usually begins by once again focusing on the previous marriage(s). The areas that generally need most examination include: feelings and attitudes of each toward the past, their former spouse(s), themselves, and their divorce(s); reasons why the divorce occurred and how they tried to avoid it; how they have changed since their divorce and how they have not changed; and why they think this marriage has more chance to survive. Certain leading questions may be helpful in this process:

- What caused you pain and/or anger in your former marriage?
- What will keep you attached to your first marriage? What will make it easy for you to put it behind you?
- Do you think you have forgiven your former spouse for the hurt and humiliation that you had to endure?
- Do you think you have forgiven yourself for the hurt that you caused?
- Can you recall good aspects of your first marriage without feeling grief, resentment, or anxiety?

Although the discussion varies radically according to the couple, the minister is primarily concerned about how they have dealt with the past, how much the past will positively or negatively influence the new relationship, the clarity of the couple's present goals in light of their past, their sense of failure, guilt, and self-esteem, and their readiness for remarriage.

One goal of this session is to help the couple begin to divorce themselves emotionally from their past marriage(s) and spouse(s), so that they do not have strong feelings of any kind regarding either. Emotional divorce in most cases cannot be accomplished in a few short sessions of counseling, but it can commence, so that the couple will feel liberated enough to be able to commit themselves more fully to their new relationship and be less affected by the past. In working through these issues, it may be necessary for the minister to meet privately with one or both partners, and possibly even refer them to a specialist in a particular area. For example, if the woman has been abused by a previous husband, she may need more intensive therapy with someone qualified in this field before being able to achieve an emotional divorce. Her prospective spouse may see the counselor also for insight into the problem as well as suggestions of ways to assist in the process of healing.

The couple may also find helpful a brief Bible study of Mark 10: 1–12 and/or the other divorce and remarriage texts. Particularly useful is the commentary on the Mark 10 passage in Eduard Schweizer's *The Good News According to Mark,* a portion of which was quoted in chapter 2.

Tom and Sarah, mentioned earlier, found this portion of the process to be very liberating. Both talked and sobbed freely about their divorces and the lack of support they had received from their families. Sarah, in fact, had been "disowned" by her parents and one sister when she sought to divorce her alcoholic husband. Of course, they would never attend this wedding, even though she would invite them, "mostly for the sake of my children." As it turned out, they did not attend, as she had predicted, and she did feel pain. However, a year after their wedding, she wrote:

> I am still estranged from my family even now. It hurts, but we're dealing with it as we always do—we love each other a little more. . . . The only way you can pull free from the past is to recognize that, first, you can't change it, and secondly, you must learn from it. The only way to accomplish both is to bring the past out in the open. Talk about the pain, laugh about the good times, but see it clearly. Couples should be encouraged to speak freely about what they expect from one another. Communication helped us to break free and realize how lucky we are now.

After the previous marriage(s) has been thoroughly discussed and resolved as well as possible, the present relationship can be further explored. The following questions are helpful:

- What is your partner's most endearing quality?
- What are some of the strengths of your new relationship?
- Are there any similarities between your partner and your former spouse? How do you feel about those?
- Do you think that you can communicate with each other about all issues?
- Are there any areas that you have a hard time discussing?
- Every couple argues sometimes; what are the things that you usually argue about?
- How do you resolve conflicts or disagreements when they come up?
- How do you go about making important decisions?

As these questions and others that may come to mind are discussed, the minister can observe how the two communicate with each other and offer insights, interventions, and suggestions as needed. Books or workshops on developing communication skills may be suggested as well. Several are listed in the section on "Suggestions for Further Study" at the end of this book.

At this point, it is important to discuss the homework the couple have prepared for this session: their lists of what they *want* and *need* from their partner and their remarriage, and how they *feel* about the partner. As with so many areas of life, in marriage and remarriage people too often set their expectations at a level that is difficult if not impossible to attain. Moreover, in relationships of all kinds expectations are held but often not communicated. Is it any wonder that marriages run into difficulty and even break down? To magnify this problem, those entering remarriage often have even higher expectations than those entering first marriages, because many desire love and security so strongly, while others were hurt so badly last time that they have given their new partner the status of a savior. In an effort to avoid severe disillusionment and disappointment later, it is important that each partner discover and share the expectations that he or she has for the partner and the relationship.

The couple's lists are a good tool for exploring these expectations, unearthing "hidden agendas," and negotiating expectations that are realistic and healthy. Each list should be examined separately, beginning with the wants. One partner volunteers to read first, after which that person is asked to clarify any wants that need further explanation. In addition, the minister might ask how well these wants are being met at present and discuss ways that the other partner or the relationship itself can better fulfill the list. In some cases, unrealistic wishes are expressed, and compromises must be negotiated. The minister can assist in this process by moving the conversation along and making sure that both partners are heard by the other, but the couple need to work out their own compromises.

After each list of wants is explored, the minister can move on to the list of needs, noting that while one hopes that a spouse and relationship will satisfy all one's wants, this does not always happen. It is critical, however, that each other's needs be met. Again, each partner takes a turn reading the "needs" list, after which clarifications can be requested by the other or the minister. Often a person's list of needs will echo the list of wants just read. In these instances, it is important that the pastor help that person distinguish which, in fact, are needs and which are only wants. Some discussion might also be needed regarding how each one's needs can best be met and how each can inform the other in appropriate ways when needs are not being satisfied. The sensitivity of the minister is essential in this part of the exercise, especially in regard to needs that are not presently being met and fears of one or both partners that certain needs will not be satisfied in the future.

In like fashion, the list of feelings is explored. While most feelings tend to be positive, it is the minister's task to watch and listen for signs of anxiety, disappointment, and dissatisfaction. Often the words are positive, but the body appears nervous, tense, or stiff. When such body language is pointed out, the inner feelings generally surface and can be explored. In remarriage situations, these feelings can often involve fears of difficulty or failure in living as a stepfamily. Many times these result from misinformation that couples have heard about stepfamilies. Therefore, this exercise also offers the minister an opportunity to educate the couple regarding some of the dynamics, myths, and realities of stepfamily living, because invariably they share some of the cultural myths about stepfamilies and have expectations that are negated by research in the field. The educational dimension of the preparation process is an essential element.

Among the topics that must be discussed are parenting and stepparenting. While many couples downplay the impact that they think the children will have on their marriage, research suggests that children are the primary cause of redivorce. The couple have no time without children, as first marrieds do, when they can nurture their own relationship. The children are present from the start, with their own needs and expectations.

During this discussion, one essential truth must be offered, again and again, until it is heard and internalized by the couple: "Your couple relationship needs to be your top priority at all times." It is difficult for couples to hear this truth, especially if they have had the major responsibility of nurturing the children for some time. They assume, and often desire, that their primary loyalty and energy should be given to parenting. Researchers, on the other hand, agree unanimously that in stepfamilies where the couple's relationship is strong, so that their discipline is consistent, the children are unable to get between them and play one against the other; and when the couple communicate regularly about the needs, problems, and concerns of the children, and do not keep secrets from each other which allow alliances to form, the children usually make a healthy adjustment to stepfamily living.

As time permits, the discussion about parenting and stepparenting can continue. In many cases, however, the subject will need to be discussed further during session three. Many areas must be explored during this important discussion:

- The natural parent's feelings and fears regarding the children and the stepparent
- The stepparent's feelings and fears regarding stepparenting, and these particular children
- Areas of agreement and disagreement regarding the rearing of the children, including discipline, values, priorities, communication, goals, the role of the former spouse and his or her family role expectations, bonding, and the like
- The myths, for example, "Stepparenting is the same as parenting"; "It is easier to be a stepparent if the natural parent is dead"; the wicked stepmother/father myth; "the 'right' family model is the nuclear family"; or "There will be instant love"
- Adoption of the children (this is an option in only a very few cases)
- Effective parenting when the children live in two households
- Typical parenting and stepparenting problems in stepfamilies such as: One or more members may have difficulty establishing a place in the family order; feelings of guilt; the desire to "make up" to the children for the upset caused by the divorce; the expectation that they can create a close-knit, nuclear family; struggles in the area of sexuality; bonding; power/control issues; sibling and stepsibling jealousy, rivalry, and bonding; loyalty struggles; communication; trust-building
- The couple's hopes and intentions regarding having children of their own
- Reaching agreement on plans for celebrating holidays and other special occasions and feelings about these plans
- Deciding which people are going to be included "emotionally" in the new family, such as former in-laws, friends from former mar-

riages, friends established during the "single" stage, new established friends of the couple, and others

During this discussion the minister should offer concerns, insights, opinions, facts, and hopes for the couple to consider; possibly suggest books for further study; raise issues for the couple or the family as a whole to discuss further; offer techniques and skills to enhance communication; and point out areas of apparent or potential conflict, encouraging further discussion and compromise.

As noted earlier, the educational dimension of the process is essential. If the new families are to be strong and healthy, they must be as informed as possible about the joys and struggles that stepfamily living offers. This education is provided in two ways: through the homework and in the sessions with the minister and children's counselor. A thorough reading of these chapters will provide the staff with much of the necessary information. However, it is strongly suggested that those using this process read one or more books from the "Suggestions for Further Study" lists at the back of this book.

Families are also educated through the various supplemental materials that this preparation process utilizes. The Workbook, "My Parent Is Getting Remarried," is designed to offer education to the children. Both the adults and the children can find counsel in the homework assigned to them at the end of session two, Helen Coale Lewis' book *All About Families the Second Time Around*. In addition, the adults are loaned two audiotapes by Elizabeth Einstein, a recognized expert in the field of stepfamily living: *The Stepfamily Journey* (1987) and *Stepfamily Living: Myths and Realities* (1985). The tapes are a valuable resource for the education of pastors and children's counselors as well.

In addition to educating families, this preparation process also encourages couples to begin creating a vision together of their life as a family unit, including the values and priorities that will guide and shape their lifestyle. A second piece of homework for session three assists the couple in this visioning process. Entitled simply "Love and Marriage," this list of eleven brief quotes will be used almost daily by the couple between sessions two and three. The minister instructs the couple to move very slowly through the statements, reading a new one only every one to three days, reflecting on it individually for as many as twenty-four hours, writing a love letter or reflection to their partner about what it means to them and to their relationship, and finally sharing the letters with each other and spending at least twenty or thirty minutes together, without others, discussing them. The pastor then continues: "At our next session, we will discuss these eleven statements. I will not want to see your letters, so make them as personal as you wish. I will ask you to share with me the essence of what you discussed in regard to each statement, and then I will share with you why I feel it is an important and valid statement. Then we can discuss each one together. In the process, I hope you will receive some thoughts, insights, and values that you can keep in the back of your mind, things that will help you maintain a strong and healthy marriage as you face the many joys and struggles of life together in the years to come."

The exercise on the following pages can be photocopied from these pages or typed up and run off on church stationery by pastors and counselors using this remarriage preparation process.

Like most couples, Sam and Betsy responded very positively to this homework: "We found the statements that you sent home with us the most helpful. They made us realize how differently we could feel about things, yet still come to similar conclusions."

This homework, along with the two audiotapes, prepares the way for the process to shift. During sessions one and two, the primary emphasis has been on looking back at the past and its impact on the present, and looking at the present dynamics of the family's relationship. The future has been discussed, but only in a minor way. Session three, on the other hand, will strongly emphasize the future of this new family and help to prepare them to face both the celebrations and the hardships of stepfamily living. To this end, the minister can ask the couple to consider their relationship in the light of this statement:

> I believe that all people, as they journey through life, are searching for wholeness. We all have gifts and strengths, and we all have weaknesses and areas that need strengthening. When we choose our mates, usually we choose someone we think can help us find this wholeness, because they are often strong where we feel weak. In other words,

I believe that opposites attract for a reason. We think that our mate will either help us grow stronger in our weaker areas, or just "fill in the gaps," so that between the two of us we will share a wholeness; "the two will become one." Between now and our next session, please think and talk about this idea and all the ways that each of you hopes that your partner can help you on your quest for wholeness.

The second session ends with a gathering of the entire family again, with the minister and the children's counselor if one is being used. After sharing briefly what each has done, along with more informal conversation, a date is set for session three. Session two concludes with the joining of hands and saying of a prayer. Following session two, the minister reflects alone, or with the children's counselor, about the session, so that session three can be planned and important material and feelings included in discussion with the adults or the children.

LOVE AND MARRIAGE

This exercise is meant to be done slowly, with no less than twenty-four hours allotted to each statement. At the beginning of each one- to three-day period, each partner should read a new quotation on the list. Then spend some time reflecting on that statement and how it applies to your partner and your marriage. Before discussing the statement with your partner, write your reflections on separate sheets. If you wish, write them in the form of a "love letter." Finally, spend at least twenty to thirty minutes together reading and discussing your letters or reflections.

1. "People need a successful marriage a lot more than they need microwave ovens and televisions."—David and Vera Mace, "Marriage in Transition," *Marriage Enrichment Resource Manual.* (St. Paul, Minn.: National Marriage Encounter, 1978), p. 97.
2. "You have to know you are loved without any fine print in the contract."—John Powell, "Dialogue and Prayer in Marriage," *Marriage Enrichment Resource Manual.* (St. Paul, Minn.: National Marriage Encounter, 1978), p. 120.
3. "Love is that condition in which the happiness of another person is essential to your own."—Robert A. Heinlein.
4. "A good marriage happens between two people who are able to entrust to each other their vulnerability . . . and who are able to appoint each other guardian of their soul. —Unknown.
5. "Sexual love is part of God's love . . . one of the most powerful forces on earth."—Virginia A. Heffernan, "Christian Sexuality: One in the Flesh, One in the Spirit," *Marriage Enrichment Resource Manual.* (St. Paul, Minn.: National Marriage Encounter, 1978), p. 110.
6. "I don't try to control a sunset. I watch it with awe as it

unfolds. I like myself best when I can appreciate another person in the same way as I appreciate a sunset."—Carl R. Rogers, "From Heart to Heart: Some Elements of Effective Interpersonal Communication," *Marriage Enrichment Resource Manual* (St. Paul, Minn.: National Marriage Encounter, 1978), p. 85.

7. "Love is a decision."—Slogan used by Marriage Encounter.

8. "One of the greatest gifts God has given is a sense of humor, or the ability to laugh at ourselves and our mistakes. Because God is a part of our marriage, we are able to laugh, for the burden does not lie completely on our shoulders."—Renel Howe, "Miracle of Dialogue," *Engaged Encounter Manual* (St. Paul, Minn.: National Marriage Encounter, 1978), p. 38.

9. "The goal of marriage is not happiness. The goal of marriage is growth."—Source unknown.

10. "When you're coasting, you're going downhill." —Gordon Ellis.

11. Read from the New Testament: 1 Corinthians 13 ("Love is patient . . .").

CHAPTER SIX

Session 3:
Looking Ahead
with the Couple

Session three begins where session two left off, with the new family together as a unit, along with the minister and the children's counselor if one is being used. This session usually feels very different from session two, however. The normal anxiety over facing something new and different is gone, most families preparing for remarriage now trust the staff and the process, and they have shared an experience that most find both interesting and enjoyable—the exercises and experiences suggested in Helen Coale Lewis' book *All About Families the Second Time Around.* In fact, most couples, and especially children, come to session three excited to talk about their experiences. It is important to give them the opportunity to do so and affirm the work they have done together. In cases where the couple and children are less enthusiastic, the minister needs to elicit their thoughts and feelings. Usually this builds their excitement.

This opening conversation is valuable because it reinforces an experience that all the new family members have shared. One of the reasons why new stepfamilies have so much difficulty at first is their lack of shared experiences, values, role expectations, and trust. In other words, they lack "history." Their time with the Lewis book not only allows them to share an experience, it helps them negotiate new roles, family rituals, nicknames, and other important ingredients of strong, healthy families.

After this initial conversation and the separation of the couple and children as outlined in chapter 3, the adults usually continue their discussion from session two on parenting and stepparenting. One way to initiate this conversation is to continue discussing *All About Families the Second Time Around.*

Somewhere within this discussion, the minister needs to reinforce the importance of the couple relationship, which was discussed briefly in chapter 5. It is here described by John and Emily Visher, two of the most prominent names in the field of stepfamily relations:

> One stepfamily goal which leads to healthy growth for all the individuals is the achievement of strong couple bonding. A strong coalition between the adult couple has been determined . . . to be a primary characteristic differentiating the psychologically most healthy intact families from less well-functioning intact families. Its importance may be even greater for smoothly functioning stepfamilies. . . . In stepfamilies secure couple bonding needs to be accompanied by flexibility of roles and acceptance of a somewhat loosely functioning family unit. (Visher and Visher 1979, pp. 208–209)

The importance of a strong, growing, cohesive couple relationship in the development of a functioning, healthy stepfamily cannot be overstated. And parents should be aware that children are usually only too happy to divide the couple. There is usually a deep desire to divide their parent and stepparent, which very often stems from a deep-seated fantasy about their natural parents reuniting.

Therefore, the next task of session three is to discuss the homework that the adults have prepared for this lesson, much of which is designed to enhance their couple bond. The tape(s) they listened to offered many important teachings regarding stepfamily living. These should be reviewed highlighting and discussing the "Five Myths of Stepfamily Living" as noted by Elizabeth Einstein on her tape *Stepfamily Living: Myths and Realities:*

[1] "The stepfamily functions the same as the nuclear family."
[2] "We'll do what we did in our first marriages, only better."
[3] "Instant love will occur between all family members."
[4] "Stepfamilies that develop out of death are easier."
[5] "The part-time stepfamily has it easier than the full-time one."

(Einstein, 1985)

For a variety of reasons, these myths of course are not true, but because they are frequently repeated, they are very often believed by people entering remarriage. It is essential that the couple learn the facts.

It is just as important to highlight and discuss the four long-term promises of remarriage and stepfamilies that Einstein outlines on the same tape:

[1] "Adults have a new chance at marriage, and children get to see a marriage succeed."
[2] "They provide additional role models to one another, and expose each other to different attitudes, values, skills, and hobbies. This exposure produces growth."
[3] "Children of divorce and remarriage tend to become more flexible and adjustable as adults."
[4] "A stepparent can have an intimate relationship with a child who is not his or her own."

(Einstein, 1985)

After discussing the tape(s) and highlighting as many learnings as possible, the couple's attention is turned to the "homework" sheet entitled "Love and Marriage," a good tool for helping the couple strengthen their bond as well as develop priorities and set goals for their relationship. It is also intended to help them develop a vision of what their marriage can become. It incorporates the dimensions of a balanced relationship between the spirit, the mind, and the body. The minister leads the couple in discussing each statement, one at a time, eliciting the couple's thoughts and reflections. Sometime during the discussion the essence of the comments following each quotation below needs to be conveyed clearly.

1. *"People need a successful marriage a lot more than they need microwave ovens and televisions"* (David and Vera Mace). We are social beings, searching for the wholeness that only close, intimate relationships can provide. But it is so easy to let our priorities become distorted. In the quest for comforts, luxuries, and material possessions, we take our relationships for granted, and then they begin to deteriorate. Very often this happens when a couple want a house so badly that they will work double shifts or opposite shifts in order to have it more quickly. Their marriage suffers as a result. Often they get the house, but they've lost something more valuable in the meantime. Sometimes the damage is irreparable. Beware: It's a temptation; we need to keep our priorities straight.

2. *"You have to know you are loved without any fine print in the contract"* (John Powell). If you've ever seen an insurance policy, you know that there's always fine print: "This policy applies, *except* under the following circumstances . . ." Well, there is no fine print attached to your vows; there are no "ifs." This contract always applies. It's permanent. And if you have any qualifications, let's talk about them now. A marriage cannot grow intimate and close in an insecure environment; that's why living together is never as difficult *or* as satisfying as marriage. The "back door" is always open; there is always "fine print."

3. *"Love is that condition in which the happiness of another person is essential to your own"* (Robert A. Heinlein). Marriage and love are about helping each other grow into the persons that we can become. And growth is fulfilling and brings happiness, even though it's often difficult and painful as it's happening. If one is stifling the other's growth, that person will not be happy, and ultimately neither will the one doing the stifling. That's not love. Probably the best way to describe it is through the example of a sexual relationship. If your partner is being cared for and loved, and being satisfied, then she or he is more likely to love you back more fully and unselfishly. If not, she or he may begrudgingly meet your needs, but it won't be very satisfying or fulfilling to either of you. And that's true on all levels

of your relationship. The growth and fulfillment, and therefore happiness, of the other is essential to your own.

4. *"A good marriage happens between two people who are able to entrust to each other their vulnerability . . . and who are able to appoint each other guardian of their soul,"* (source unknown). This is something that is never-ending. It is continually growing toward a deeper and deeper intimacy with each other. This is the most important goal of marriage, and one for which we can, and should, always be striving. Picture it this way: Picture taking out of yourself those parts of you that are most vulnerable: the hurting parts; the fearful parts; the parts you are ashamed of and embarrassed by; the parts that someone could hurt you with, or maybe even destroy you with. Take them out and hold them in your hand. That's what I would call your "soul." Now, give it to your partner, knowing that she or he could hurt you very badly by laughing, or making fun of you, or using them against you in an argument. It's not easy and it never will be. Marriage is growing more and more intimate, so that you're able to entrust more and more of your soul to your partner, knowing that she or he is not going to use it against you or hurt you with it, but hold it carefully and return it to you at least as good, maybe even a little better, than when you let go of it. But realize that this goal is never fully accomplished, because each one is continually discovering more and more of what is inside himself or herself. Therefore, there's always something new to discover about your partner. This is what keeps marriages alive and growing, happy and fulfilling, for years and years—in fact, for a lifetime— growing ever more intimate and deeper in love. I hope that you will keep this goal in the back of your mind always.

5. *"Sexual love is part of God's love . . . one of the most powerful forces on earth"* (Virginia A. Heffernan). I view sexuality as a gift from God, to be enjoyed and used as a way to show our love for someone and enhance our relationship. However, it is powerful, and I'm sure I don't need to tell you how many relationships have been helped or destroyed because of sexual issues. Nothing will destroy a marriage as quickly as extramarital affairs, abuse, incest, or other sexual

issues. So, I warn you: think carefully before you get involved in anything like that.

More importantly for our purpose here, it's good to remember that sexuality is also powerful in the relationship between two people. Sexual relations are so intimate and vulnerable that we can really help or really hurt our partner's self-esteem very quickly by what we say or do. Again, please use sex as the gift it can be; use it to enhance your relationship, and to build up your partner's self-image.

6. *"I don't try to control a sunset. I watch it with awe as it unfolds. I like myself best when I can appreciate another person in the same way as I appreciate a sunset"* (Carl R. Rogers). If you are thinking that once you get married to your partner you'll be able to change him or her and certain habits or patterns that bother you, be careful. That's a trap. More often, what bothers you now is going to bother you a lot more then. We really don't have that much control over our spouses, and if we try to, it usually only fosters resentment. Instead, we can encourage growth, help our spouse to see a vision of whom he or she can become, and support him or her in achieving it, but not much more than that. The same is true in our relationship with children and stepchildren. This is somewhat of a "trick question," however, because if our spouse is developing some very destructive habits, like getting heavily into alcohol, for example, we would be silly to stand by and do nothing, even though we still cannot control him or her. So this is a difficult issue, and one in which you need to use a lot of good judgment or even seek out counseling help. I believe that every marriage has periods when counseling would be very helpful and growth-providing, sometimes even necessary. I hope you will feel free to come back to me or, if you wish, to seek out another counselor should the need arise. It will shortcut a lot of trial and error, and help you keep your marriage strong.

7. *"Love is a decision"* (Marriage Encounter). This is a catch-phrase in Marriage Encounter, and it is true. But most people have a hard time with this idea because they think of "love" as a feeling. Think of it instead as an action. If it is an action, then we can decide to do or say the loving thing in any given circumstance. If you both

come in from work feeling tired, impatient, and upset, and all you want to do is just yell and scream and throw pots and pans at each other, one of you can decide to do the loving thing, which in this case might be to put your own needs "on hold" for a moment, listen to the other, and be supporting and loving. This, in turn, frees up your partner to do the same for you.

On the other hand, sometimes doing the loving thing means getting upset and being tough, pushing your spouse to take more responsibility, or whatever else the situation implies. Just keep in mind that at any given moment in your marriage, you can decide to love. This is also true in parenting and stepparenting. Continually be asking yourself: What is the most loving thing I can do in this situation? And remember, what is most loving needs to be considered for the long run, not just for the moment. Sometimes it is difficult to consider the long-term implications, but we need to continually.

8. *"One of the greatest gifts God has given is a sense of humor, or the ability to laugh at ourselves and our mistakes. Because God is part of our marriage, we are able to laugh, for the burden does not lie completely on our shoulders"* (Reuel Howe). The message here is the conviction that there is a third party involved in your marriage: God. And if you keep nurturing your faith, you will always understand and realize that God is a part of your marriage. Because of that, the burden is not all on your shoulders. If, in the face of a major problem, we thought that it was entirely up to us to solve it, we would feel so overburdened that we would lose our perspective and our sense of humor. However, when we realize that the burden is not entirely on our shoulders, that allows us to live through, and grow through, some very difficult, even horrendous, problems and trials with our humor and optimism intact. It also allows us to be able to live with, and even laugh at, the mistakes that we are bound to make along the way. Therefore, it is essential to keep your faith growing and strong.

9. *"The goal of marriage is not happiness. The goal of marriage is growth"* (source unknown). Happiness is a by-product. We are

happy when we are growing and feeling fulfilled. Therefore, I urge you to look for ways to keep your marriage growing: marriage enrichment, marriage encounter, courses, special times for just the two of you, counseling, leisure activities, and dialogues about your feelings, thoughts and beliefs. And what I mean here is not just your growth as a couple, but also each one's individual growth. Growth is what brings happiness, and growth is really the goal of marriage. Living in a stepfamily situation, your growth as a couple is even more essential, because the bond that the couple has is the key to the ongoing strength of the entire unit. Over and over again research has proven that. Your relationship has to be more important than the children and everything else. Otherwise there will be very many outside forces and internal pressures and stresses working to divide you. Growth is a very difficult goal, but an essential one.

10. *"When you're coasting, you're going downhill'* (Gordon Ellis). It is so tempting and easy to coast, to take your relationship for granted and to think you don't have to work on it. But just remember that the moment you begin to coast is the moment that the relationship starts going downhill. It is very tempting to get so caught up in the day-to-day duties and responsibilities, especially of your job or parenting, that you let your marriage "slide." That is a trap. Your marriage is still going to be there long after the children are off on their own and you're retired from your job. So keep it alive, dynamic, and growing. Don't let it stagnate.

The same is true in your relationship with other family members. It is important to make time and to work hard at relating to your children and stepchildren. Good, healthy relationships require lots of attention and care. The entire family will suffer if either of you starts to coast.

11. *Read from the New Testament: 1 Corinthians 13 ("Love is patient . . .").* Paul's message about love is beautiful but difficult, even in marriage. And actually the Greek word that he is using here is *agapē*, which basically means a love that we offer to all people just because they are children of God. This kind of love is really difficult, isn't it? Well, I see marriage as a training ground for this kind of

agape love. If you can make that kind of love a goal for your marriage, and if you can experience it between the two of you, then you can begin to share it with others. You cannot contain love; it has to be shared. There's an outreach dimension of every good marriage. So, again, I lift it up as a vision for you to work on and strive for, within your marriage and beyond.

After completing discussion of the eleven statements on the "Love and Marriage" sheet, the minister can remind the couple of the "wholeness" concept presented to the couple at the end of session two. First, elicit from the couple their thoughts and reflections about the concept, encouraging them to think more deeply, even now, of additional ways that they hope and expect their partner to assist them in their quest for wholeness. It is important to remind them, however, that two "whole" individuals must be their goal if their marriage is to be healthy. So often, one person's personality is smothered in a marriage, and that is not what this wholeness concept implies.

If time remains, any unresolved issues from previous discussions or other areas that need to be addressed can be dealt with now. Depending on what has been considered in the course of conversation, these might include role expectations, duties, bonding, responsibilities, parenting/stepparenting, financial considerations, sexuality in the home, spiritual compatibility, and the like. If the allocated time has passed, such issues can be dealt with at the beginning of session four, before creating the wedding ceremony.

Before completing session three with the couple, the minister needs to reflect personally for a moment on how well the goals of the counseling portion of the remarriage preparation process have been met thus far. The primary goals of counseling with the couple are to help them resolve some of their feelings regarding the past that may hamper them in the future; to educate them about and prepare them for the joys and struggles of stepfamily living; to teach them stronger, more effective communication and negotiation skills and techniques; to strengthen their couple bond; to explore their expectations and to assist them in making their expectations more realistic; to help deepen their faith in a redeeming God; to give them a good feeling about counseling so that they will be more likely to seek out help when they need it in the future; and, it is hoped, to strengthen their ties to the church.

If any of these goals have not been addressed, the minister may wish to work on them before the session ends or, more likely, schedule another session to do so. With most couples, however, the four-session model is sufficient. Ministers and counselors should be cautioned that the goal of this process is not to counsel individual family members, or the couple, through disabling grief, unhealthy addictions, or deep personality disorders. Referrals are made when more serious issues and diagnoses such as these arise. Although it may be legitimate to add a session or two, depending on the family and their needs, it is also important for the minister to keep the goals and limitations of the process in mind.

If a couple needs continued work in one or more areas, it is always an option to have them come back for more counseling after their wedding or to refer them to a good therapist for more long-term therapy later. In any case, it is very important to let them know that they are encouraged to come back after they are married, whenever they need assistance working out an issue or problem. This not only helps them through a period of struggle; it also binds them more closely to the church. Bud and Lesley are only one example of many. Bud has never been involved in a church; Lesley grew up Roman Catholic, but was not active during or after her first marriage. They came to our church primarily for Lesley and her parents, who felt strongly about having a "Christian marriage." After their wedding, they returned for the "six-month checkup" that we had joked seriously about. Soon after that, Lesley returned for help working through a problem they were having. In the meantime, Lesley began attending services regularly and soon volunteered to teach church school. From that, she joined the Christian education committee. She wrote even before she joined the committee:

> Until meeting and talking with you, I attended church very erratically. (Catholic services at that!) I always felt that I'd like to begin attending church on a regular basis again. I missed that. I went often when I was a child. After meeting you and seeing the type of person you were I thought I'd like to attend one of your services. It was great! Of course you know what's followed. Thank you for that! I haven't lost hope that

Bud will attend. He likes you and your services and the way things are done. I'll keep working on him!

By the end of session three, the bulk of the counseling portion of the process has usually been completed. If the process has accomplished its goals, couples will echo what Sandra, whom we met in chapter 1, wrote upon reflection, after she and her family finished their preparation:

The most helpful part of the preparation process was the frank discussions about the things that bothered us about each other. We did learn how to communicate better. Without your initiation of these matters, these issues probably would not have come up calmly and dispassionately, but would have been the source of irritation or arguments later. Our decision to marry each other was, by the end of your preparation process, a very informed one.

Session three concludes with a gathering of everyone again and a discussion of how everyone is feeling about the process so far. Then the homework for session four is assigned: working together, using wedding ceremonies from a variety of denominations and other sources along with the original remarriage materials found in chapter 8, to develop an appropriate, unique, and special wedding ceremony. While the couple will usually choose many of the parts of the service themselves, they may plan to include the children in the entire process if they wish. In either case, there are several opportunities when they need to involve the children in decisions, such as whether the children will be members of the wedding party, as, for example, ushers, bridesmaids, flower girls, or ring bearer; whether they will come up to the chancel or altar area with the couple for any portion of the service; whether they will take any type of vows in the ceremony, and what those vows will be; whether they will sit in the church, and whether or not they will sit with stepsiblings; whether or not they will be named in the pastoral prayer; and other roles they might have at the wedding or reception, such as acolytes, guest-book attendants, or some other part. Children should be included in discussions and decisions regarding these specific areas of the service. The building of the ceremony is an opportunity for the family to communicate with one another, to work together on a common project toward a common goal, to affirm the importance of one another in both the service and the family, and to strengthen the bonds between them. It is meant to be enjoyable. It is also meant to be life-giving in the sense that one of the themes and feelings that have been dealt with in counseling can now be expressed liturgically and publicly—feelings, fears, hopes, confessions, absolution, and faith. After brief, informal conversations, session three is concluded as was session two, with hands joined as a prayer is offered.

CHAPTER SEVEN

The Counseling Process
with the Children

As the remarrying couple joyfully prepare for their wedding, they may
be blind to, or fail to understand, the mood and behavior of their
children. It is important, however, to take the children seriously
because the health of the remarriage in many ways depends on
them. Twelve-year-old Melissa was a good case in point. She was
angry that her mother, Mary, was marrying Eric. They would have
to move out of her grandparents' house to a new town. Besides, Eric
had never had kids: "What does he know about being a father?" Her
mother, who was also at this session along with Melissa and Eric,
looked at me and said, "Do you see what I mean? She's impossible!
I don't know what we're going to do."

I looked at Melissa, who had never known her real father or any
home but her grandparents', and commented that if I were Melissa,
I "might sound angry, but actually I'd be scared to death of all the
changes." Melissa's face softened immediately, and soon she began
to sob. Mary began to move toward her, but Eric stopped her and
he went himself. She cried on Eric's shoulder for several minutes,
and then looked at him thankfully. "Don't worry," he said. "It's
going to be all right. We'll make sure of it." I then said to Melissa:

"You know, Melissa, there's an old proverb that says, 'We may forget those with whom we've laughed, but we never forget those with whom we've wept.' I think you and Eric may get along just fine." Melissa nodded. Less than a year later, she made an appointment with me to discuss being adopted by Eric. Shortly after that, it was a reality.

Children have very strong feelings about both the remarriage of a parent and the divorce of their natural parents. In fact, bringing in a stepparent often reminds them of and intensifies their longing for their absent biological parent. Most children experience some degree of loyalty conflict, often rejecting stepparents in order to be "loyal" to their absent parent. Not surprisingly, the older a child is, the more likely this rejection is to occur. The rejection may not be as verbal as in Melissa's case. More often, in an effort to be a "good child," a youngster may exhibit the rejection of a stepparent by setting up situations that create conflict between the couple and force them to take sides. Children almost always win such a conflict, which reinforces the point made earlier about the importance of keeping the couple's relationship strong and communicative. The rejection of a stepparent may also take the form of acting-out behavior at home, school, or elsewhere. A child's grades may begin to plunge. Fighting, stealing, lying, and other attention-getting behaviors may become frequent.

This rejection often works. In most cases of divorce following remarriage, some researchers estimate 90 percent, the children are identified as the primary cause of tension and conflict. However, it is important to remember that the children are not motivated by cruelty. They are grieving, confused, and afraid, and usually unable to acknowledge or express those feelings, even if they have anyone around with whom they feel comfortable enough to share them.

Therefore, including the children in the remarriage preparation process helps them feel listened to, understood, and taken seriously. Whether the minister or a children's counselor works with them, the major tasks are to listen to and acknowledge their trauma; to help them grieve the loss of their natural family; to relieve their guilt regarding their feeling of responsibility for their parents' divorce; to teach them as much as possible about what living in a stepfamily involves; to assist them in identifying other feelings regarding divorce, remarriage, parents, stepparents, siblings and stepsiblings, and others; to affirm their "place" and importance in the new family; to acknowledge and repudiate some of the myths of stepfamily living, such as the "wicked stepparent," "instant love," and others; to discuss and help alleviate their loyalty conflicts; to offer them a method for communicating with parent and stepparent regarding new family rules and situations so that their input will be heard and valued; to inspire them to build bonds with new family members so that the family unit will be strengthened; to motivate them to think creatively and optimistically about the positive aspects of stepfamily living; and to bridge the emotional gap between the adults and the children at the time of the remarriage by offering each party some awareness of what the other is feeling.

These goals are addressed by using two tools as a basis for both discovering issues and guiding the flow of the counseling process. The first tool is the workbook "My Parent Is Getting Married" (see Appendix). The second is Helen Coale Lewis' excellent children's book *All About Families the Second Time Around*. There are several important reasons why I have chosen this particular book:

1. Of all the good children's literature on the subject that I have examined, it offers the most complete and realistic educational discussion.

2. It lends itself to use by an entire family. Therefore, they not only share the unifying experience of working together on it, but also it leads them in making decisions together about many dimensions of their life together, so that everyone's opinions are considered. In addition, it offers them a common language and framework from which they can speak and function as well as raising their joint consciousness with regard to prevalent pitfalls and myths that handicap stepfamilies and/or their members. Finally, it openly reassures the members, especially the children, that the remarriage does not mean that they must instantly love one another or give up their attachment to loved ones from previous families.

3. It takes into account and encourages the children's deep need to keep a strong relationship with their noncustodial parent. As

Claudia L. Jewett asserts in her book *Helping Children Cope with Separation and Loss*:

> The success of the new relationship does not depend on the fading of the memory of the earlier one. . . . A child may feel conflicting loyalties if he thinks he must turn his back on his old caretaker before he can share affection and intimacy with a new one. The helping adult must respect the child's need to maintain ties to a noncustodial parent while devising ways to help the child understand that you can have a parent-child relationship with more than one parent or set of parents." (Jewett 1982, p. 137)

4. It leads the family in developing its own new rituals and traditions, one of the ways, as research has shown, to give strength to stepfamilies.

Another resource may be substituted for this book if the counselor or minister locates, or is more comfortable using, a different one. Using these tools, the minister or counselor needs to be very sensitive to what the children are feeling and work quickly to build trust with them. Sharing his or her feelings and fears, along with stories about his or her own life and family, can enhance this process.

As outlined in chapter 3, all the children of the couple ages four through seventeen are invited to the remaining sessions. This approach may possibly create an odd mix, bringing together as many as four to six children with a wide age span, some of whom will live with the new couple and others who will only visit for overnights, weekends, and/or vacations. While the goal is to help this group communicate, negotiate, and build trust with one another, there may be occasions when the goal cannot be accomplished for some reason. The minister or counselor will then need to decide whether the goal can be accomplished more effectively by separating certain age groups, individuals, or family units. It may also be the case that one or more of the children will exhibit such angry, antisocial, or depressed behavior that the minister or counselor will feel very uncomfortable. It may be necessary in such cases to make referrals to a counselor who has more specialized experience and/or qualifications. As is always the case, referrals should be made with extreme care and sensitivity and followed up regularly. The minister or counselor is not likely to know what alterations are needed in the process, however, until session two is well under way.

In counseling children, it is essential to bear in mind the ages of the children, because children of different ages respond differently to both divorce and remarriage. While this process is not really designed for preschool children, older preschoolers are invited for the sake of fostering family unity. Preschoolers were not included in the design on the basis of research provided by Judith S. Wallerstein and Joan B. Kelly in the landmark study of the children of divorce documented in *Surviving the Breakup: How Children and Parents Cope with Divorce* (New York: Basic Books, 1980). This research found that following a divorce young children regress behaviorally and become very needy for affection and attention. However, with a loving, sustaining relationship through this period, they normally react positively. After remarriage, providing that there is an absence of adult strife in the home, preschool children tend to be accepting of the new stepparent. The research also indicates that with preschoolers more positive changes usually occur as a result of working with the adults in the family rather than with the preschool children themselves.

In contrast, school-age children five to twelve are expected to benefit the most from this process and it was primarily developed for them. These children tend to be much more open about their feelings. Therefore, for counseling purposes, they are much easier to work with. (See Visher and Visher, 1979.)

Within this age span, however, there are some important differences to keep in mind. Five- and six-year olds, for example, are quick to deny anger and other feelings that have been labeled "bad," or to reverse their feelings; for example, "I'm not mad at Daddy; he's mad at me." They also might interpret one parent's leaving as if it were a death. From ages five through seven, children also exhibit difficult feelings through symptomatic behavior such as overeating, fighting, or other manifestations.

Children between eight and twelve years of age generally find support outside the home, primarily from peers, and may express an intense anger at the situation. Often they assume the behavior of the absent parent, complain of bodily aches and pains, and adjust poorly in school. These children, as well as younger school-age children, also struggle with what to tell their friends about their new family. It does not seem to matter that one third of the children in many schools and classes live in stepfamilies. They still tend to feel outcast and different, and need to regain their perspective and self-confidence.

The gender of children at this age also makes a difference. School-age boys are likely to identify with their fathers and maintain strong loyalties to Dad. They accept a father's remarriage much easier than a mother's. This may be due to their viewing their new stepfather as a rival for Mom's affection. Conversely, girls at this age have a much harder time accepting a father's remarriage. If the divorce of a child's biological parents occurred during the time of the child's second oedipal phase (ages nine to fourteen), not only is the child apt to feel rejected by the most important man or woman in his or her life, but also the child tends to feel guilt over causing the breakup. In order to relieve this guilt and to attempt to restore the original parents' marriage, the child may be determined to break up the new marriage (and often succeeds). In addition, children at this age may feel very reluctant to invest themselves emotionally in a new stepparent after having been "rejected" by a biological parent. While these are all difficult issues, this remarriage preparation process and follow-up can be successful with children ages eight to twelve primarily because of their openness with regard to their feelings and their ability to grow to trust the minister or counselor, as well as, ultimately, the new stepparent.

Erin, at age eleven, was a textbook case of such a child. Like most children, she had closely monitored her biological parents and their attitudes over the six years since their divorce. Both remained extremely important to her, and her self-image was closely tied to both. All the experts agree that an ongoing close relationship with both biological parents is the key to adjusting to their divorce and growing from it in a positive way. Unfortunately, Erin's father had paid little attention to her. In fact, he was often downright cruel to her, promising to visit and never showing up, ignoring her on birthdays and Christmas, and being very erratic about even contacting her. Often a year or more passed without even a phone call. Like most children of divorce who are treated with such rejection, Erin was unable to counter-reject her father. Rather, she idolized the man, acknowledging to me that it was more the "father of her dreams" than her real father whom she loved so dearly. Erin's dilemma was a loyalty conflict. While admiring and loving her stepfather, Tony, who wanted very much to adopt her after his marriage to her mother, Alicia, Erin was afraid to get "too close" to Tony for fear of "hurting" her natural father. Although she wanted to be adopted, she feared that it would preclude any further chance of getting the love and attention that she craved from her natural father. This dilemma had surfaced as she prepared for her mother's remarriage, coming as a surprising revelation to Erin. Unfortunately it could not be resolved at that time, and two years later she was still struggling with it. It was usually triggered by the mention of adoption, or by some form of contact by or about her natural father. Each time it surfaced, she visited me again.

While in some ways the outcome is less important than the fact that Erin dealt with the problem in an open, honest, and healthy manner, she ultimately decided that her good relationship with Tony was not dependent on being adopted. She could feel comfortable being his "daughter" without carrying his name, and could still hope for the day when her father would "love and accept" her. With encouragement, she was able to discuss her feelings with Tony, who proved to be very understanding and supportive of her decision, and showed no sign of being hurt as she had expected.

While preteens can be helped a great deal, teenagers are far more difficult to help. The process can be helpful, however, especially for young teens. There are several reasons for this difficulty. First, teens tend to deal with feelings of loss by withdrawal and cynicism (Visher and Visher, 1979). Second, adults are often insensitive to their natural need to assert their independence, and often become authoritative, which leads to strife and hostility in the home (Visher and Visher, 1979). Third, the teenagers may well be trying to break up the marriage, as suggested earlier, in order to relieve their own guilt feelings over the breakup of their biological parents. And finally, also as suggested for the younger age group, they may be attempting to avoid getting hurt again by refusing to invest themselves emotionally in a relationship with the new stepparent. This is not to say that they cannot be helped; they can be and are. There are simply more barriers. Therefore, they may require a separate session, and usually conversation replaces the use of the Workbook. Working with the parents to consider "normal" teenage characteristics and needs, as well as the above specific needs of stepchildren, can also prove helpful.

The children's counseling portion of the remarriage preparation process is an integral and sensitive part of it. Two basic assumptions undergird the work with children in this remarriage preparation process. Both are summarized powerfully by Judith S. Wallerstein and Sandra Blakeslee in the book *Second Chances: Men, Women and Children a Decade After Divorce*, an update of the Wallerstein and Kelly 1980 study. In the new book's conclusion, they write:

> Almost all children of divorce regard their childhood and adolescence as having taken place in the shadow of divorce. Although many agree by adulthood that their parents were wise to part company, they . . . suffered from their parents' mistakes. . . . Many of the children emerged in young adulthood as compassionate, courageous, and competent people. Those who did well were helped along the way by a combination of their own inner resources and supportive relationships. (Wallerstein and Blakeslee 1989, p. 298)

There is no denying it: a divorce is difficult and it leaves its mark on children. Nevertheless, living in a stepfamily can be a positive and life-giving experience. This counseling process is designed to help children minimize the long-term negative effects of divorce while maximizing the long-term positive effects of remarriage and stepfamily living.

The first session with the children, as outlined in chapter 3, begins with the entire family gathering with the minister and, if participating, the children's counselor. After this initial period, the children meet separately from the couple, which both encourages honesty and affirms the importance of their feelings and thoughts. The first task of this session with the children is to restate why the children have been invited to participate. They are valued by their parents, and, like their parent and soon-to-be stepparent, they need to prepare for this remarriage and the new family that will result from it.

One way to do this, as well as to introduce the Workbook the children will be using, "My Parent Is Getting Remarried," is to give each child a copy of the Workbook and read to them "A Note to the Child." This Workbook is printed in its entirety in the Appendix of this book, and permission is granted for ministers and counselors to photocopy as many copies of it as they need for use with the children in this remarriage preparation process. In this first session, chapters 1 through 3 of the Workbook are used.

It is also helpful, at this point, to discuss confidentiality. Assure the children that nothing they say will be shared with their parent and/or almost-stepparent without their permission or request.

This session with the children focuses primarily on the divorce of the children's natural parents and their feelings about the divorce(s). It is designed to help the children better understand marriage and divorce and realize that the divorce was not the fault of the children (an important realization for many children of divorce); acknowledge the changes in their lives as a result of the divorce, as well as their feelings about these changes; deal with their fears of being hurt when they dare to develop closeness with others again; and mourn the loss of their noncustodial parent, which may be the most important goal of all, because all children grieve about their parents' divorce. Moreover, because children do not move as quickly as adults through the stages of grieving that Dr. Elisabeth Kübler-Ross has identified—denial, guilt and anger, bargaining, depression, and reorganization—parents tend to negate or minimize their children's grief. As a result, a major problem for children in most remarried families is incomplete mourning. Helping the children grieve is, therefore, a central goal of this preparation process.

Sarah, mentioned previously, affirmed this goal when she wrote to me, following her remarriage to Tom, about her children's experience in the preparation process: "Do you know that my kids never cried about the divorce until they met with you? They're the same as adults in this situation. They have to get over the pain and frustration of divorce, and adjust to this new family unit. They have to be encouraged to speak out about what they're feeling."

"My Parent Is Getting Remarried" is designed to address this goal. As the Workbook is shared, the minister or counselor should read aloud, letting the children read along from their own copies (or, if comfortable, just looking on as the counselor reads), stopping to fill in blanks, answer questions, and so on, as called for. Their answers are to be shared with the counselor, who will listen compassionately and sensitively and discuss the responses with them. Throughout the process, the minister or counselor may stop to address issues and concerns that arise, even if that slows down the completion of the process so that a special session for the children must be arranged.

Dealing with the past and their feelings about it with a caring counselor, through the use of the Workbook, is extremely helpful. As one children's counselor noted:

> The success of Jimmy's counseling experience was obvious when in his final session he identified the most helpful things he had learned. . . . He wrote "When your parents get divorsed[sic] . . . it's not your falt-[sic]." Jimmy's parents divorced when he was four. At nine, Jimmy recognized that their divorce had nothing to do with him. No one had told Jimmy that his parents' divorce was caused by him; in fact, the opposite was true. Jimmy had for years, however, felt responsible. In counseling, Jimmy learned that divorce is never the fault of the child. He saw it in print, we talked about it, and he came to believe it. The guilt Jimmy had been carrying around for years was eliminated.

Later in her report about Jimmy, she continued: "Jimmy came to recognize that exploration of his feelings helped him understand himself better."

Before the first session with the children ends, it is important to bridge the gap between looking at yesterday and today, the work of this session, and looking ahead at what is to come as the children embark on the adventure of living in a stepfamily. Chapter 3 in the Workbook, "My Parent Is Getting Remarried," along with the homework it assigns in *All About Families the Second Time Around*, is designed to bridge that gap. It often helps when introducing it to tell children that at least three U.S. presidents were stepchildren: George Washington, Abraham Lincoln, and Gerald Ford. Older children may be intrigued to find out that Jacqueline Kennedy Onassis and author Alex Haley also had stepparents. The fact that the book *All About Families the Second Time Around* is a gift from the church to their family also excites many children. They can enjoy coloring the pictures and completing the worksheets, as well as sharing it and doing its exercises with the family, even their other biological parent who is not involved with the wedding, providing the remarrying parent does not object. The key, of course, is to interest the children in reading the book and taking its exercises seriously, so that it can serve as another tool to help them learn about the drawbacks and gifts of stepfamily living. The book should be brought back to the next session.

After a brief period for reflecting together with parents, almost-stepparents, and minister about the discoveries of this session and the homework for the next session, the children join hands in a circle of prayer with the others. During this brief prayer of thanksgiving and petition, the minister gives thanks for this session, naming particular discoveries and happenings, and prays for the insight, wisdom, patience, and understanding of the whole family unit as they prepare for the upcoming remarriage and the stepfamily living that will result from it.

When the children return for their next session, the minister or counselor spends a few minutes with the entire family, as outlined earlier in chapter 3. During this time general comments and reflections are solicited from any or all of the members regarding their homework in Helen Coale Lewis' book. Feedback is also requested about the process as a whole thus far. Following this brief opening of the session, the children remain to continue their work with the minister or children's counselor while the adults move to another office either to work with the minister or to wait for the minister to finish with the children. Chapter 4 of the Workbook (see Appendix) is used to guide the children in reflecting on their learnings, thoughts, and feelings regarding their family's homework in the Lewis book. At this point, many issues concerning the stepparent and/or stepsiblings are likely to be raised. The counselor or minister needs to be on the alert for them and discuss them as they arise. Another important function of this portion of the process is to help the children realize specific ways in which they can (and do) hinder and enhance the functioning of the stepfamily, primarily by "playing the games" that Lewis describes, such as the "good old days" game, and making their parent the "middleman" to the stepparent. In so doing, the counselor tries very subtly to motivate the children to work for the stepfamily rather than against it.

Another important discussion to pursue with the children is their feelings about the sharing of "family history" and "what you want your new stepparent and stepsiblings to know about you." Not only does this exercise foster sharing between members of the new family and help them get to know one another better, it also helps to unify them, if not by sharing a common history, at least by sharing a common knowledge of each other's history.

Discussing the fact that love grows is also essential. Though it is a common myth regarding stepfamilies, there is no "instant love" among the members, and parents and children quite naturally have a stronger love for their biological family members, at least in the early years. This came as a surprise to Jimmy, whom we met earlier in this chapter. His counselor, in fact, wrote following her work with him:

> Jimmy believed the myth of instant love. When we first discussed that Becky probably loved her children more than she loved him, Jimmy was shocked. His eyes opened wide, his eyebrows shot up, and his body tightened. Love grows; it takes time to learn to love—that made sense, but the words that seemed to relax Jimmy were that his dad probably loved him more than he loved Becky's children. By the time he had to respond to Gordon's statement of love, Jimmy was able to say he felt "fine" because "my father had more time with me and Becky had more time with Chris and Keli."

In conjunction with this discussion about love, the minister or counselor also needs to explore the children's fear about what loving their stepparent might mean in terms of their love for their other natural parent. Does it make them disloyal? And do the children worry about losing some of their natural parent's love because of the new stepparent?

Finally, it is essential to explore with the children their "special event days," with regard to both their former family and their new stepfamily, and to make sure that they discussed both while doing their homework with their new family. The sharing of these helps the family (1) understand what is important to each member; (2) begin the long-term process of negotiating what is kept, what is discarded, and what is blended; and (3) commence the all-important task of creating a common history with shared rituals and traditions.

Chapter 5 of "My Parent Is Getting Remarried" continues to try to motivate the children to work at enhancing the new family unit. Basically, it encourages them to be honest about their needs and feelings; to be patient, because it takes time and hard work for any family to become healthy and happy; to be sure to seek help if they need it, either at the church or somewhere else; and to help make the remarriage ceremony special and important to all by sharing their opinions when it is being planned and by participating in it in a positive, loving way on the actual wedding day.

The inclusion of the children in the ceremony is a critical dimension of the process. As Sandra, whom we have mentioned before, noted:

> You met with my son, Chad, who was nine years old at the time. He spoke about you in positive terms, and understood that the sessions were to help ensure a happy future family life. . . . We think that it was essential that he was involved in the preparations and planning for a new family commitment. He and John have always had a wonderful relationship, and, thank God, it has continued to grow. . . .
>
> We totally enjoyed personalizing our ceremony. More important than our choices of readings or music, though, was the inclusion of my son in the ceremony, and the vows he exchanged with his new dad. Chad still refers to the wedding as "our" wedding, the day "we" married each other.

Because it is so important to include the children in the ceremony, their homework for the final session is to work with the couple, at least minimally, depending on their age, interest, and time constraints, in creating the remarriage ceremony. The extent of their involvement, of course, must finally be determined by the couple, but they have been counseled by the minister during this third session to make sure that their children are included in the process, at least in the creation of their parts in the ceremony. Chapter 8 will outline how this is accomplished.

This session with the children ends like the last one, with a time of gathering the entire new family unit with the minister and maybe the children's counselor, the sharing of highlights, remaining counseling work to be done, and homework for the next session. Finish with a prayer of thanksgiving and petition.

CHAPTER EIGHT

Session 4:
Creating the
Remarriage Ceremony

The final piece of the remarriage preparation process is the creation
of a unique and personal remarriage ceremony by the couple, their
children, and the minister. There are several reasons why this portion of the process is just as important as the counseling dimension.
First, it offers the new family another shared memory. Because all
the family members enter this new family with separate histories
and memories, and because the collective memory of any family provides strength to it, the memory of creating this ceremony together
and sharing in it will be a lasting and life-giving one. It will become
a building block for their new life together.

Secondly, ceremonies and rituals have been developed by soci-
eties throughout human history as a way of legitimating the
entrance of people into new groups and new life phases. They
have a sanctioning power for people that is important to provide,
especially in light of the controversial nature of remarriage.
Rituals have also been designed to help people make major life
transitions. The remarriage ceremony obviously does that for the

couple and their children, as they move into a new and different kind of family living.

Creating and participating together in the remarriage ceremony can also provide the family with a model not unlike an architect's miniature layout of a new building or campus. Family members can utilize it in the future as together they attempt to meet the struggles and the joys of daily living. It becomes one of their first acts of sharing together in a life event.

Finally, and most importantly, this portion of the process is essential because, as Ronald L. Grimes notes so poignantly in "The Need for Ritual Practice": "No matter how deeply couples 'share' in retreats or learn, under priestly guidance, to 'talk through' everything, they are not prepared to be wed until their insights are 'somatized,' made flesh, in ritual" (Grimes 1984, p. 10). The issues, feelings, needs, hopes, fears, and faith that have been so much a part of their counseling sessions need to be enfleshed in the drama of Christian worship, so that the good news of the Christian gospel, the life-giving message of God's forgiving and redeeming love, can reach deeply into the lives of this family and congregation to offer healing, hope, and new life. The entire process logically and emotionally moves toward an act of worship, a celebration of the Easter faith, which empowers this humble but hopeful couple as they dare to stand again at the altar and make new promises before God.

Some would say that remarriage does not belong in the church. Some would even say that marriage does not belong. There have always been such voices in the church. Martin Luther was one of them. He believed that matrimonial affairs belonged to the jurists and not to the church. Historically, however, Christians have increasingly affirmed that the wedding ceremony is an act of worship. From the earliest days, Christians have asked the leaders and pastors of the church to bless their marriages, and as they did the dogma of marriage as a sacrament gradually developed. By the twelfth century, this dogma was fully developed, yet it was not until 1563 at the Council of Trent that Christian marriage officially became a religious ceremony. Protestants soon reacted, and for them marriage ceased to be a sacrament. In spite of Martin Luther's plea, however, they still regarded it as a divine institution, a rite of the church, an act of worship.

Remarriage too is an act of Christian worship, because it is

the glad response of total persons, "heart, soul, strength, and mind" to the saving acts of God in history. It is the communal and personal celebration . . . of God's love for creation and for every human being. This Divine love is revealed in God's gracious covenant with the people of Israel and in God's coming into the world in Jesus Christ.

Christian worship is more than a passive response to God's revelation. It is itself a pentecostal proclamation. It both answers and announces the good news of God's love for all the world and invites all persons to share God's saving embrace. (United Church of Christ, 1982, p. v)

In order to help make the ceremony become such a responsive act of worship, the minister works very closely with the family, and primarily with the couple, to create a unique and special ceremony that meets their individual needs.

As the basis for planning the ceremony, I have created a workbook which I lend to families to take home following session three for their use in preparing for session four. This workbook, which I have entitled "The Wedding Workbook: Resources for Creating Your Wedding Ceremony," is used by both remarrying couples and those marrying for the first time. The workbook is divided according to the various components included in a wedding ceremony: Opening Remarks, Calls to Commitment, Prayers of Invocation, Statements of Intention, Blessings of the Parents/Families, Secular Readings, Scripture Readings, Sample Homilies, Marriage Vows, Exchange of Rings, Pronouncements, Pastoral Prayers, Benedictions, and Special Touches. In addition, there is a special section of service parts designed just for remarriages, entitled "Resources for Remarriages." Within each section, many options that I have gathered over the years are offered to couples. After studying the possibilities in a given section, the couple may choose to use one as it appears, to change one, to combine portions of two or more, or to write a new one with the minister's assistance. When they have chosen the wording of their ceremony, the couple then decide about use of such optional components as musical solos, hymns, service bulletins, the sacrament of the Lord's Supper, the lighting of a wedding candle, and others. All this planning is done as homework between sessions three and four, and is as inclusive of the children as possible, depending on each couple's need and their children's ages and interests. When they return for session four, they go through their choices of service parts with the minister to check wording, flow, and overall content. At this time the Wedding Workbook is returned to me for use with future couples and families.

Although remarrying couples can and do use many of the same service parts as those marrying for the first time, who also use the Wedding Workbook, they also have their own special needs that must be met. When ministers use the same service for both, as is often the case, they neglect to meet these important needs. When this happens, responsive worship is often stifled rather than enhanced. For genuine worship and praise to occur, the confusing and/or negative feelings prevalent in the couple and/or the congregation at such an event must be addressed. There needs to be open and honest recognition of people's feelings, the failure of the previous marriage(s), the need for repentance and forgiveness, fears about the new marriage relationship, and the importance of the children from previous marriages. The love and forgiveness of God must be witnessed to in a way that is real and meaningful to those present. At the same time, the church's commitment to the intention of God in the institution of marriage must be proclaimed.

The section of the Wedding Workbook entitled "Resources for Remarriages" attempts to meet these special needs through the inclusion and wording of various service parts. One of the most important parts is the homily written by the pastor for the wedding of a specific couple. Because homilies are prepared differently for each wedding, they can be written with the history and needs of that particular family in mind. The homily provides an opportunity for the pastor to speak to the couple and their guests concerning issues, fears, and difficulties that still need to be addressed; to place the remarriage, and the preceding divorce(s), into the context of our Christian faith; and to offer a foundation of faith on which the couple/family can build in the future.

For example, the following homily was used in the remarriage ceremony of Frank and Helen, whom we met in chapter 3:

> Frank and Helen, at the top of the bulletin for this special service today I put a quote—a quote that came to mind as I pondered your wedding ceremony and what I would say to you and to your friends and family today. The quote reads: "The story of the Christian is the story of many resurrections" (John Calvin).
>
> You know, in some ways it seems like just yesterday when I, along with many other people here, shared with each of you some very painful, agonizing times. And, though each of you had different circumstances surrounding your pain, both of you experienced what I would call "crucifixions" in your lives—horrible, destructive crucifixions—crucifixions that would destroy many people.
>
> And yet, to look at you today, one would hardly know it. You come here today so full of life, so full of love, so full of joy. You know, it's almost like witnessing a miracle. Indeed, it's like seeing a resurrection! And it's so beautiful!
>
> But *why?* Why is it that such crucifixions would destroy so many people's lives and yet in yours there's a resurrection? Why? Well, I'd like to remind you of the words that Jesus said to so many people who found healing when they came to him. He said: "It is your faith that has healed you."
>
> Frank and Helen, your faith has, indeed, healed you. You see, for so many people the crucifixions are the last word. And so, seeing no hope for more than that, they remain crushed and broken and burdened.
>
> However, your faith has told you that the crucifixions are not the last word—that God has the *last* word. And your God is the God who was made known to us in the person of Jesus Christ—a God of love, a God of forgiveness, a God of hope, a God of new life, a God of creation and re-creation, a God of resurrection; a nurturing and caring God, who *always* has the last word, and who is always at work, making resurrections happen in the lives of those who allow them to happen, as well as those who have "eyes to see them."
>
> Frank, over the past few years, during Dot's long illness, and since her death, I have watched you rely on your faith in this loving God. And I have seen you put your life, and your agony, into God's hands. And God has healed you! Instead of wounds, I now see scars. Instead of brokenness, I see new life. And it has been beautiful to

watch, my friend. In fact, you stand as a model for so many of us, who yearn to have faith like yours. Yes, Frank, your faith has healed you.

And, Helen, over the past year, I have watched you grow, and find a deep faith. And it really feels good to think that I, and this church family, and certainly Frank have been of help to you as you have discovered a loving and forgiving God, and as you have journeyed in your faith, so that you can trust, and find new life in the hands of that God. It's wonderful! It's precious! It's a resurrection!

Yes, the two of you come here today like two flowers growing out of the ashes of your past hurts, and celebrating the new life, the resurrection, that God has brought forth into your lives.

Well, it is your faith that has healed you. And it is your faith that has brought you once again to this altar. And on this, your wedding day, all I want to say to you is, "Keep that faith. Don't ever let go of it, no matter what crucifixions you face in the future."

That faith will make your marriage strong and alive and vital. And with it, you will prove again and again, as you have already, that "the story of the Christian is the story of many resurrections." Amen.

Another extremely helpful aspect of services of remarriage as we plan them here is the inclusion of children from previous marriages. Sometimes this is done by making the children attendants of the bride and groom. In other weddings, they are invited to share their own vows, promising that they will do their best to help make their new family successful. This should be done with extreme caution, however, because it may cause guilt feelings later if the children are unable to fulfill their vows. At other times, the stepparent(s) and stepchildren promise to accept one another into their lives, and to attempt to grow in understanding, care, and love. This, too, should be done with great care. The minister may wish, during the fourth session, to work with these family members to develop the appropriate wording for such a vow.

I am reminded of the case of Matthew and Steven (ages thirteen and eleven) and their soon-to-be stepmother, Betty. The boys did not like Betty; they did not hide that fact. She had "never had kids," and "she keeps Dad away from us." Betty did not have much use for the children, either; that was obvious by the way she spoke with and about them. In separate sessions the minister attempted to help each side see the situation through the eyes of the other, acting as an interpreter and "bridge." While Betty and the children did not build a strong relationship during counseling, defenses were lowered and an opportunity for one was created. By the last session, both sides felt comfortable enough with the other to sit down together and work out very carefully with the minister the wording of the following vows that they exchanged at the ceremony:

> **Minister:** Betty, in marrying Joseph, you are also becoming the stepmother of Matthew and Steven. Will you do your best to be a good, loving and faithful stepmother?
>
> **Betty:** I will.
>
> **Minister:** Matthew and Steven, you have heard the vows taken by your father and Betty. As they live out these vows, Betty will become your stepmother. Do you promise to support her in her efforts to be a good stepmother?
>
> **Matthew and Steven:** We do.

Other possible vows for children, parents, and stepchildren from several sources are included in the Wedding Workbook. Another example is:

> **Minister** (to child or children): _____, you have heard your parents (or your mother/father and _____) make a very profound, yet very joyful, promise to each other. As a witness to this solemn event, do you promise to support them in fulfilling God's will for their lives together, and for your life together as a family? If so, answer: I do.

Regardless of how the children are included, it is important to include them. This not only affirms their importance in the life of the new family that is being established, but it also helps them let go of more of their resistance to the remarriage by allowing them to have a vested interest in its success. Finally it makes the relationship between the stepparent(s) and stepchildren a public and formal one.

Clearly, one of the most effective strategies for this part of the process is having families develop the service together. This allows them to word the ceremony in such a way as to consider the needs of all. In cases such as the one involving Matthew, Steven, and Betty, it is extremely important to be able to develop a ceremony that honestly takes each person into account. This can set the stage for future honesty, which can deepen and enhance their relationships within the family.

Developing their own ceremony together also helps the family's bonding process. As Sandra noted in chapter 7: "More important than our choices of readings or music, though, was the inclusion of my son in the ceremony, and the vows he exchanged with his new dad. Chad still refers to the wedding as 'our' wedding, the day 'we' married each other."

It must be remembered, however, that while it is essential to include the children, there must be a limit to their inclusion. The ceremony is designed to allow two adults to make important, solemn, and lifelong promises to each other. Their couple relationship must be distinct from the stepfamily relationship as a whole. While both partners need to be aware that children are "part of the package" when they marry, the children also need to be aware that there is a private and intimate dimension of the couple relationship in which they are not included.

There are two other very important components of Christian worship that can be used very effectively in services of remarriage, the elements of confession and absolution or assurance. These can be used not only with the couple, but also with the congregation and family, who often come to a remarriage ceremony feeling guilt, hurt, disillusionment, and fear. A moment of confession often helps people to confront and deal with their negative and confusing feelings. A statement of absolution or assurance following confession serves to highlight the church's message of forgiveness and grace. These elements allow the couple symbolically to "die" to their past sin or failure, and to find new life trusting God's grace and love. This, of course, is the essence of what remarriage is all about.

Out of the ashes of the past arises new life for those who can hear the liberating word of a loving and redeeming God, offering them freedom from the chains of guilt, anger, despair, and hatred. Confession and assurance/absolution can be a very powerful and integral part of a remarriage ceremony. For example, the confession might read as follows:

> **Minister** (to the couple): Our Lord Jesus called us to repent: to acknowledge our guilt, confess our sin, and trust in God's grace. _____ and _____, before you make your marriage vows to each other, I call you to confess your failure in your previous marriages, to express your willingness to put away your old vows, and to trust God's forgiveness and healing grace in this new relationship. Therefore, I ask you now, in the presence of God and these witnesses: Will you confess your own complicity in the broken vows of the past? Will you publicly release those vows and that relationship in order to live completely in the vows you make today? And will you trust God alone for forgiveness and renewal?

> **Couple:** We will.

> **Minister** (to congregation): At this remarriage ceremony, it is important to realize that it is not just this couple who need the love and forgiveness of God. Each of us, as family and friends of these two, share in the guilt of their broken vows. In addition, we have often failed to be loving, taken family and friends for granted, failed those we love, and taken our own vows and promises lightly. Therefore, will the family and friends here gathered now confess your own faults and failings, and will you trust God to forgive you?

> **Congregation:** We will.

Following the confession, one of the following assurances of pardon, or another of the minister's choice, may be used:

1. **Minister** (to all): We are a people who are forever doing things, saying things, and thinking things that build walls of separation between us and others, between us and God, and even within ourselves. And of our own accord, it is impossible to break down these walls. However, these walls are not the final verdict on our lives. The final verdict comes in the form of a Word. We meet that Word face-to-face in Jesus Christ. And that Word proclaims that we are loved with God's everlasting love, that we are of infinite value and worth. Standing in that Word, and that Word alone, I would dare to declare to you that you are forgiven, that you have been received and made whole. This is God's doing. Let us rejoice and be glad in it. Amen.

2. **Minister** (to all): Hear these words of forgiveness that we receive from Saint Paul in his epistle to the Romans: "Who is in a position to condemn? Only Christ, and Christ died for us, Christ rose for us, Christ reigns in power for us, Christ prays for us" (Romans 8:34, Phillips). In Christ, we are forgiven and made whole. Thanks be to God. Amen.

Other service parts may be designed for remarriage ceremonies as well. For example, a call to commitment in a remarriage ceremony might read as follows:

Minister (to the couple): _____ and _____, as you contemplate the meaning and importance of marriage and the vows that you are about to make to each other, I am sure that you are deeply aware of your first marriage. That marriage failed. Today, I charge you to let go of that old relationship, and to dedicate yourselves, wholly and completely, to this new relationship. Remember, as Christians we affirm that it is God who gives you to each other and offers you this new opportunity to develop a meaningful and lasting marriage relationship. We are an Easter people, and remarriage can be seen as a symbol of resurrection and new life. As Jesus came forth from the tomb of death into new life, so, out of the ashes of your former marriage, you are offered new life this day. Therefore, give yourself fully, one to the other, in both good and difficult times ahead, and you will know the renewal of life that God offers you this day.

A prayer of invocation might read:

Gracious God, always faithful in Your love for us, we rejoice in Your presence with this couple. Help them to give themselves, each to the other, in love and trust. And make them know your forgiveness of their broken commitments in the past, that they might die to that past and open themselves to the new life you now offer them. We pray in the name of our Lord and Savior, Jesus Christ. Amen.

The exchange of rings can also be designed especially for a remarriage ceremony:

Minister (to the couple): What do you give in token and pledge of the vows here made? (Bride and groom give rings to minister) The wedding ring is the outward and visible sign of an inward and spiritual bond which unites two hearts in endless love. May the rings that you now exchange with each other be seen not only as symbols of your love for one another, but also as symbols of the new life which your remarriage offers to each of you.

Groom (placing the ring on the bride's hand): _____, I give you this ring, in token and pledge of our constant faith, abiding love, and new life in marriage.

Bride (placing the ring on the groom's hand): _____, I give you this ring, in token and pledge of our constant faith, abiding love, and new life in marriage.

Finally, as a conclusion to the remarriage ceremony, there is another very moving symbol which can enhance the blending of the new family. After all the vows have been shared, the rings exchanged, and the public pronouncement of marriage offered, when the only fitting response that a couple can make is to kneel in humble and hopeful prayer before the God who bears witness to their covenant, the children are invited to join hands with the prayerful couple. Then the pastor's hand is placed on top of the two closest hands, as a pastoral prayer such as the following is offered on their behalf.

O Lord, our God, accept our prayers and expressions of joy and thanksgiving for the love that _____ and _____ have found in each other, and for the promise they share in their life together. Guide and strengthen them, we pray, that they might fulfill the covenant they have made here today. Guide and strengthen them, we pray, that they may grow, as persons and as partners, to the fullness of their capacity. Guide and strengthen them, we pray, that they might learn to trust: themselves, each other, and you. Guide and strengthen them, we pray, that they might be good, loving, and faithful parents to _____. O Lord, be with them through all the joys and struggles that lie ahead, that both may deepen and strengthen their marriage relationship, and that this family may grow stronger and more productive and loving day by day. May their remarriage be a symbol to all of a new life that begins today, beyond the pain of their past. O Lord, we pray these and all our prayers in and through Jesus the Christ, our Lord and Savior, who taught us to pray together, saying, "Our Father . . ." (The sources of portions of this prayer are unknown.)

This concluding act is a moving and meaningful tool for the uniting of the family, as is the ceremony as a whole. As noted earlier in this chapter, rituals have a sanctioning power in society. When families are able to create their own ceremony, they are able to make public feelings and fears that could later be destructive and receive the support of family and friends that they will need in the future.

Tom and Sarah wrote after their ceremony: "We were able to show the world how right we were for each other, in our own words. We both felt as if we were proclaiming to everyone—'Look, we've made our mistakes, but now we've got it all together.' Our ceremony gave us that start on the right foot."

The event of the remarriage ceremony is the final dimension of this process for remarriage preparation. It is also its culmination. Remarriage ceremonies provide wonderful opportunities for the church to offer an assurance of God's grace and love to a group of people very much in need of it. These people are then allowed to embark on their second marriages without being plagued by the mistakes of the past, and with a new sense of hope and promise for the future.

The remarriage ceremony, therefore, can be a powerful tool for strengthening stepfamilies, and through this process remarrying families can make their ceremony memorable, unique, and life-giving. The remarriage ceremonies that have been created by those who have tested this process for remarriage preparation have been beautiful and moving, and each has been different. Some of them have had more emphasis on confession and absolution; others, on educating their family and friends. Some have included their extended families; most have heavily incorporated their children. All of them, however, in one way or another, have included strong and powerful testimonies to the renewing and transforming resurrection faith that our Christian heritage offers.

Back in 1970, Myron Madden, in *The Power to Bless*, criticized and challenged the church in this regard:

> Modern [people] find [themselves] in need of reassurance that bestows wholeness. . . . Meaningful religion speaks of rebirth and . . . blessedness. In order to come to blessing, [people] need to be freed from the feeling of curse. By maintaining an uneasy silence when couples remarry, or denying a Christian ceremony to those who affirm the notes of confession and penitence for their first failures, and hope

and grace for the new marriage, the church contributes to that curse. It is time for the church to recognize the reality of Christian remarriage, and to offer its blessing by use of such a ceremony. (Madden, 1970. p. 15)

Today, more than two decades later, the same criticism and challenge are still valid. They are answered, however, by the many beautiful, moving, and life-giving ceremonies that can be created as part of this remarriage preparation process, strong foundations for the building of new lives and new families.

CHAPTER NINE

Conclusion

What I have presented thus far is a process for preparing families, both couples and their children, for remarriage in the church. My hope is that pastors will use it and find it extremely helpful in their ministry. My fear, however, is that some will think that this process will "thoroughly" prepare families for remarriage, and that no further problems will arise and no other ministry will be needed. It may be very tempting for some ministers to believe this, especially if they have been searching for a quick, easy solution to the dilemma of preparing couples or families for remarriage. This is an illusion. It is impossible in a few short hours and sessions to prepare a family thoroughly for the many pressures that await them in stepfamily living. Many potential problems will be eliminated, others shortcut, but many more will come to them. It normally takes three to five years for stepfamilies to adjust to their new lifestyle.

The purpose of the process is not to eliminate this difficult period of adjustment, but to foresee it and affirm its necessity, to help shorten it, and to offer the family tools for coping with it and growing stronger through it. While the process will initially decrease the time that the minister spends counseling stepfamilies because they will be better prepared for their adjustments, it will not eliminate that time because stepfamilies will also feel more comfortable in seeking out the minister's help when problems arise. In addition, like any other quality "product," it will become popular. Knowing where help is to be found, other stepfamilies and couples seeking remarriage after divorce will seek out the minister and church "who helped their friends." The demands on time will ultimately increase, but so will the effectiveness of the church's ministry to the large and growing population who are affected by divorce and remarriage just as it has in the Seekonk Church, where this process was created. The positive response to it by the Seekonk Congregational Church offers evidence of the success of the project in this regard. The Seekonk Church members not only lovingly provide this process for remarriage preparation to families, along with the books and resources that it requires, but they also encourage both of their pastors to provide counseling assistance to stepfamilies, and readily embrace stepfamilies into the church community.

The statistics offered in chapter 1 give evidence to the Seekonk Church's commitment to providing a ministry with stepfamilies, as do the many efforts by the church school staff to accommodate the needs of children who spend one half or more of their Sundays away from church school visiting other parents and relatives. In addition, the church has recently offered the following courses: "What the Bible Says About Marriage, Divorce, and Remarriage," "Learning to Step Together," a course for adults living in stepfamilies, and "STEP: Systematic Training for Effective Parenting." A special resource library of books, tapes, and videos on divorce and remarriage was recently created. Two ongoing, lay-led S.D.R.W. (Separated, Divorced, Remarried, and Widowed) support groups meet biweekly, one for anyone and the other for people under forty years old. Simultaneously, similar support groups are offered for the children of S.D.R.W. participants. While led by Seekonk Church members, these groups are networked ecumenically with the S.D.R.W. office of the Roman Catholic Diocese of Providence, Rhode Island, which offers regular leader-training opportunities, up-to-date resources, guest speakers, and a monthly newsletter for all participants, with interesting, informative articles and a listing of all regional S.D.R.W. support-group meetings. In addition, for two consecutive years the Seekonk Congregational Church has sponsored a community-wide, daylong conference on family life, entitled simply "Families." This conference includes a well-known keynote speaker and over twenty workshop selections (from which participants choose two to attend), with professional leaders in various dimensions of family living, including aspects of divorced and remarried life. Approximately two hundred people have attended "Families" each year.

The Seekonk Church, therefore, is now offering a multifaceted ministry with divorcing, remarrying, and remarried families. The process for remarriage preparation is only one program among many, as it should be.

With the new theological understandings of the church's role and response in regard to divorce and remarriage, which I have shared in this volume, my prayer is that all Christian churches everywhere will expand their ministry to these families, as the Seekonk Church has.

For Christian people and communities, the biblical message carries power for transforming and renewing life. This process of remarriage preparation includes a faithful and pastoral interpretation of the Scriptures that is powerfully affecting both the Seekonk Church and those who come to it in search of a loving, life-giving ministry. It is my contention that other pastors and churches can use it in the same way to create a wonderful, life-giving, multidimensional ministry with this ever-increasing segment of our nation's population, thereby serving as the faithful instruments of God's love that we are called to be as the body of Christ. This implies the education not only of pastors, but also of congregations. People need to know that such a ministry is faithful to the gospel and even called for by the gospel. Then they can confidently and lovingly open themselves and their churches to families experiencing divorce and remarriage; hear their needs and respond creatively with ministries, programs, and missions that will faithfully meet these needs; demonstrate tangibly the love and forgiveness of God; and build up the body of Christ.

In conclusion, I would say that I began creating this process out of a sense of inadequacy with regard to a specific area of my ministry. Because I had never experienced divorce or remarriage, but lived happily with my first and only wife and family, I felt totally unprepared to help the growing number of divorced families who began approaching me requesting remarriage in the church. I was unsure of my theological stance and less sure of my emotional stance. My only knowledge about stepfamilies was the "bad press" they have received from fairy tales like "Cinderella." But one day as I was reading "Cinderella" to my daughter, I realized that there is one element of the fairy tale that is usually overlooked. That is the fact that the stepfamily did, in the end, reconcile and even learn to like one another. The wicked stepmother and ugly stepsisters finally repented and happily attended Cinderella's wedding to the prince. At that point, I decided that I would investigate the biblical and theological considerations of divorce and remarriage, learn as much as I could about stepfamilies, and attempt to develop a process by which I could more effectively minister to their needs and prepare them to meet the challenges ahead. Soon thereafter, I came to realize that stepfamilies may have difficulty working out their new relationships but they too can live as "happily ever after" as any of us. Of course, they do not have a "fairy godmother" or "handsome prince" to come to their rescue. They have to work long and hard at it themselves. But they do have a loving church community that can offer them acceptance, care, friendship, support, counseling, teaching, and growth. And, more importantly, they have a redeeming and renewing God, who is capable of transforming crucifixions into resurrections, pain into joy, death into new life.

My prayer, as I complete this book, is that God will use it in this redeeming work of love, and that by participating in it many remarrying families might find the new life that God so graciously offers. As the great theologian Paul Tillich wrote:

> Resurrection means the victory of the New state of things, the New Being born out of the death of the Old. Resurrection is not an event that might happen in some remote future, but it is the power of the New Being to create life out of death, here and now, today and tomorrow." (Tillich 1956, p. 24)

List of Works Cited

Efird, James M. *Marriage and Divorce: What the Bible Says.* Nashville: Abingdon Press, 1985.

Einstein, Elizabeth. *The Stepfamily Journey.* Living Series. (Audiotape.) Ithaca, N.Y.: E. Einstein Enterprises, 1987.

———. *Stepfamily Living: Myths and Realities.* (Audiotape.) Ithaca, N.Y.: Pilgrimage Productions, 1985.

Einstein, Elizabeth, and Linda Albert. *Stepfamily Living: Preparing for Remarriage.* Ithaca N.Y.: E. Einstein Enterprises, 1983.

Family Service America. *The State of Families, 1984–1985.* New York: Family Service America, 1984.

Francke, Linda Bird. *Growing Up Divorced: How to Help Your Child Cope with Every Stage—from Infancy Through the Teens.* New York: Fawcett Crest, 1983.

Furnish, Victor Paul. *The Moral Teachings of Paul.* Nashville: Abingdon Press, 1979.

Grimes, Ronald L. "The Need for Ritual Practice." *Liturgy: Celebrating Marriage.* Journal of the Liturgical Conference 4.4 (1984): pp. 10ff.

Grunlan, Stephen A. *Marriage and the Family: A Christian Perspective.* Grand Rapids: Zondervan Publishing House, 1984.

Jewett, Claudia L. *Helping Children Cope with Separation and Loss.* Boston: Harvard Common Press, 1982.

Lewis, Helen Coale. *All About Families the Second Time Around.* Atlanta: Peachtree Pubs., 1980.

Mackin, Theodore, S.J. *Divorce and Remarriage*. Ramsey, N.J.: Paulist, 1984.

Madden, Myron. *The Power to Bless*. Nashville: Broadman Press, 1970.

Monkres, Peter R. *Ministry with the Divorced*. New York: Pilgrim Press, 1985.

National Marriage Encounter. *Engaged Encounter Manual*. St. Paul: National Marriage Encounter, 1978.

National Marriage Encounter. *Marriage Enrichment Reference Manual*. St. Paul: National Marriage Encounter, 1978.

Schweizer, Eduard. *The Good News According to Mark*. Atlanta: John Knox Press, 1970.

Tate O'Brien, Judith, and Gene O'Brien. *A Redeeming State: A Handbook for Couples Planning Remarriage In The Church*. New York: Paulist Press, 1983.

Tillich, Paul. *The New Being*. London: SCM Press, 1956.

United Church of Christ. *Proposed Services of Marriage*. New York: Office for Church Life and Leadership, 1982.

Visher, Emily B., and John S. Visher. *Stepfamilies: Myths and Realities*. Secaucus, N.J.: Citadel Press, 1979.

Wallerstein, Judith S. and Sandra Blakeslee. *Second Chances: Men, Women and Children a Decade After Divorce*. New York: Ticknor & Fields, 1989.

Wallerstein, Judith S., and Joan Berlin Kelly. *Surviving the Breakup: How Children and Parents Cope with Divorce*. New York: Basic Books, 1980.

Suggestions for Further Study

Pastors and counselors using this process, as well as interested laypeople including remarrying couples, need to acquire as much knowledge as possible in the fields of divorce and remarriage. Here are brief lists of important researchers and authors in several different topic areas.

DIVORCE, REMARRIAGE IN THE CHURCH

Callison, Walter L. "Divorce, the Law, and Jesus." *Your Church,* May-June 1986, pp. 20–25. An excellent, brief, very readable word study of the Gospel texts on divorce and remarriage.

Efird, James M. *Marriage and Divorce: What the Bible Says.* Nashville: Abingdon Press, 1985. A concise, well-written, and easily understood study of the biblical texts on divorce and remarriage. If you have time to read only one, read this one.

Kelly, Kevin T. *Divorce and Second Marriage: Facing the Challenge.* New York: Seabury Press, 1983. A helpful book for churches on the divorce and remarriage dilemma. An excellent educational tool.

Luck, William F., Jr. *Divorce and Remarriage: Recovering the Biblical View.* San Francisco: Harper & Row, 1987. A long and thorough study of the biblical texts on divorce and remarriage. It is not for most laypersons, but very informative for pastors who have time to read it.

Mackin, Theodore, S.J. *Divorce and Remarriage*. Ramsey, N.J.: Paulist Press, 1984. An extensive study of the history of the church's response to divorce and remarriage. While very thorough and informative, it is more than most pastors need or want.

Monkres, Peter R. *Ministry with the Divorced*. New York: Pilgrim Press, 1985. A good, practical tool for pastors and churches developing such a ministry.

Morgan, Richard Lyon. *Is There Life After Divorce in the Church?* Atlanta: John Knox Press, 1985. An excellent, well-written challenge to pastors and churches, with many practical tools and ideas.

DIVORCE, REMARRIAGE, AND THE SOCIAL SCIENCES

Einstein, Elizabeth. *The Stepfamily: Living, Loving, and Learning*. New York: Macmillan Co., 1982. Her classic work. Einstein is one of the most knowledgeable and prolific authors in the field today. Her work is very good for both pastors and laypersons, including remarrying couples. I regularly use her booklets and tapes, available from E. Einstein Enterprises of Ithaca, N.Y.

Francke, Linda Bird. *Growing Up Divorced: How to Help Your Child Cope with Every Stage—from Infancy Through the Teens*. New York: Fawcett Crest, 1983. A good self-help book for parents and stepparents.

Pasley, Kay, and Marilyn Ihinger-Tallman, eds. *Remarriage and Stepparenting: Current Research and Theory*. New York: Guilford Press, 1987. An excellent compilation of articles with recent statistics, research, and theories about remarriage, stepfamilies, and stepparenting.

Visher, Emily B., and John S. Visher. *Stepfamilies: Myths and Realities*. Secaucus, N.J.: Citadel Press, 1979. If there is a classic piece about stepfamilies, this is it. For those who can read only one of these books, this is the one. The Vishers are the recognized experts in the field, with many important books and articles in print.

Wald, Esther. *The Remarried Family: Challenge and Promise*. New York: Family Service America, 1981. An excellent long and thorough work for counselors of stepfamilies. It may be too long and involved for many pastors, but those who read it will find it invaluable.

Wallerstein, Judith S., and Sandra Blakeslee. *Second Chances: Men, Women and Children a Decade After Divorce*. New York: Ticknor & Fields, 1989. The result of an ongoing study of divorced families, this book is destined to be, like Judith Wallerstein's previous book, coauthored with Joan B. Kelly, *Surviving the Breakup: How Children and Parents Cope with Divorce* (New York: Basic Books, 1980), the "Bible" for counselors and others who work with stepfamilies, and particularly with the children in stepfamilies. Laypeople find parts of it helpful, but overall it is too technical for most.

DIVORCE, REMARRIAGE, AND CHILDREN

Berger, Terry. *A Friend Can Help.* Milwaukee: Raintree Pubs., 1974.
———. *How Does It Feel When Your Parents Get Divorced.* New York: Julian Messner, 1977.
———. *Stepchildren.* New York: Julian Messner, 1980. Three helpful children's books by this author.
Berman, Claire. *What Am I Doing in a Stepfamily.* Secaucus, N.J.: Lyle Stuart, 1982. An excellent little book for elementary-age children, which helps them explore some of their feelings about entering a stepfamily.
Blume, Judith. *It's Not the End of the World.* New York: Bantam Books, 1980. A favorite among late-elementary-age children, Blume in this book helps youngsters cope with divorce in their family.
Bradley, Buff. *Where Do I Belong? A Kid's Guide to Stepfamilies.* Reading, Mass.: Addison-Wesley Publishing Co., 1982. I almost used this book instead of Lewis' book for the preparation process. However, it does not include families the way Lewis' book does. This is an excellent book for children.
Brown, Marc, and Laurene Krasny Brown. *Dinosaurs Divorce: A Guide for Changing Families.* Atlantic Monthly Press, 1986. This is a good tool for families experiencing divorce.
Fassler, David, Michele Lash, and Sally B. Ives. *Changing Families: A Guide for Kids and Grown-ups.* Burlington, Vt.: Waterfront Books, 1988. This guide is excellent for families facing a variety of changes and transitions, not just divorce and remarriage.
Gardner, Richard. *The Boys and Girls Book About Divorce.* New York: Bantam Books, 1971.
———. *The Boys and Girls Book About Step-Families.* New York: Macmillan Co., 1979.
Another important researcher and author in the fields of divorce and remarriage, particularly in regard to children. He has many articles in print, as well as these two helpful children's books.

Getzoff, Ann, and Carolyn McClenahan. *StepKids: A Survival Guide for Teenagers in Stepfamilies.* New York: Walker & Co., 1984. One of the few books for teens available.

Ives, Sally B., David Fassler, and Michele Lash. *The Divorce Workbook: A Guide for Kids and Families.* Burlington, Vt.: Waterfront Books, 1985. Excellent for families in divorce.

Lewis, Helen Coale. *All About Families the Second Time Around.* Atlanta: Peachtree Pubs., 1980. The best guide I've found for those preparing for remarriage and stepfamily life.

Mayle, Peter. *Divorce Can Happen to the Nicest People.* New York: Macmillan Co., 1979. The best children's book I've found for preschool and early-elementary-age kids who are experiencing divorce in their families.

Phillips, Carolyn E. *Our Family Got a Divorce.* Ventura, Calif.: Regal Books, 1979.

———. *Our Family Got a Stepparent.* Ventura, Calif.: Regal Books, 1981. Two excellent books for young children.

Seuling, Barbara. *What Kind of Family Is This? A Book About Stepfamilies.* Racine, Wis.: Western Publishing Co., 1985. Good for young children to help them explore their fears and feelings about stepfamily living.

Vigna, Judith. *Daddy's New Baby.* Niles, Ill.: Albert Whitman & Co., 1986.

———. *She's Not My Real Mother.* Niles, Ill.: Albert Whitman & Co., 1986. Two good volumes for young children on the issue of stepfamily living. They are particularly helpful for children trying to sort out their fears and feelings.

Williams, Margery. *The Velveteen Rabbit.* New York: Avon Books, 1975. A classic children's story about new life and new beginnings. A must for young readers experiencing divorce and/or remarriage in their families.

COMMUNICATION SKILLS

Currier, Cecile. *Learning to Step Together: A Course for Stepfamily Adults, A Manual for Leaders.* Baltimore: Stepfamily Association of America, 1982. An excellent course that can be used with couples or groups of couples. Communication and negotiation skills are taught from the viewpoint of stepfamily living. This is also a good educational tool for stepfamily adults with regard to the unique nature of stepfamilies.

Luecke, David L. *The Relationship Manual: How to Diagnose, Build, or Enrich a Relationship.* Columbia, Md.: The Relationship Institute, 1981. This superb workbook can be used with couples or groups of couples to strengthen their entire relationship, not just their communication skills. It contains helpful exercises for couples to use at home, along with discussion material for groups. I highly recommend it.

Miller, Sherod, et al. *Straight Talk: A New Way to Get Close to Others by Saying What You Really Mean.* New York: NAL Penguin, Signet Books, 1981. My favorite resource for helping couples enhance their communication skills. It is easy to read and understand, yet very effective as a self-help book.

Appendix
My Parent is Getting Remarried:
A Workbook to Help Children
Prepare for the Remarriage
of a Parent

The following Workbook has been developed by the author for this remarriage preparation process to serve as the basic tool with which the minister or children's counselor can help the children, both custodial and noncustodial, prepare for the remarriage of their parent(s). Portions of the Workbook are to be used in conjunction with Helen Coale Lewis' book *All About Families the Second Time Around.* Each child in the family is given his or her own copy of the Workbook, while the family as a whole receives a single copy of the Lewis book. These are provided by the church.

The workbook is meant to serve as a guide. The minister or children's counselor may venture from it if important issues need to be examined further and discussed with the children.

Ministers and counselors may photocopy this Workbook as needed for use with children in the remarriage preparation process.

My Parent is Getting Remarried

A WORKBOOK TO HELP CHILDREN PREPARE FOR THE REMARRIAGE OF A PARENT

Gordon E. Ellis

Contents

A Note to Professionals and Parents   W-2

A Note to the Child   W-3

1 Marriage, Separation, and Divorce   W-4

2 Divorce and Feelings   W-10

3 Something to Do at Home   W-15

4 *All About Families the Second Time Around*   W-16

5 What Now?   W-22

Portions of this Workbook must be used in conjunction with the book *All About Families the Second Time Around*, by Helen Coale Lewis, illustrated by Jill Dubin (Atlanta: Peachtree Publishers, Ltd., 1980).

A Note to Professionals and Parents

The remarriage of a parent, custodial or not, is a crisis time in a child's life. "Crisis," here, carries its ancient Chinese connotations of both "danger" and "opportunity." Though it is normally a time of intense and difficult feelings, it can also be an occasion for significant growth and maturity in a child's life. While positive growth cannot be assured, its likelihood can be increased if a child is assisted in preparing for the remarriage by a sensitive, understanding,and caring adult. The purpose of this workbook is to provide a remarriage preparation tool for children that can be used with professionals and parents. I do not recommend allowing children to use it alone. For maximum benefit, it should be used as a means for bringing a child's questions, fears, feelings, and concerns to the surface for further discussion in a nonjudgmental, supportive environment.

The first two chapters of the Workbook are based on the assumption that before a child can prepare for the remarriage of a parent and its implications, the experiences of the separation and divorce of his or her biological parents must be explored and the feelings regarding it resolved as much as possible.

All About Families the Second Time Around, by Helen Coale Lewis, is the basis for Chapters 3 and 4 of this Workbook. This is one of the most helpful books available for families who are preparing for, or experiencing, the early phases of remarriage. It also provides an opportunity for children, parents, and stepparents to get to know one another better and work on remarriage issues together to enhance the bonding process. Follow-up work with the children is important, however, and this Workbook offers a tool for that work.

Copies of *All About Families the Second Time Around* may be ordered separately or in bulk from:

Helen Coale Lewis,
c/o Atlanta Area Child Guidance Clinic
2531 Briarcliff Road, N.E., Suite 215
Atlanta, GA 30329, (404) 636-5875

A Note to the Child

One of your parents is planning to get remarried soon. That means that you will have a new stepparent. It also means that, in some ways, your family will be different than it has been. Your parent and "almost-stepparent" are getting ready to be remarried. They call it "preparing," and it takes a long time. There are many things to talk about and decide. Because they love you, they want you to prepare too.

This Workbook is a gift for you. It can help you prepare. We know that doing this will be painful sometimes, but it will also be interesting and fun. You will learn something every time you use it. It will help you understand more about yourself, your parents, and your friends.

1. Marriage, Separation, and Divorce

When two adults love each other and want to live with each other always, usually they get married. Getting married means that they promise to love each other, to live with each other, and to try to make each other happy. Sometimes it is hard to live with someone else, because everyone is different. When people are married, they try to live with each other even when it is hard. They talk about things they don't agree on, and they try to solve their problems together. Usually this makes them love each other more and become happier together. But sometimes people are just too different and they cannot agree, no matter how hard they try. They don't feel loved or happy, and maybe they argue a lot. Some couples even fight and hit each other. When one or both of them become really unhappy, sometimes they decide to separate, which means that one of them will move to another home. If they have children, this is very painful for the parents and the children. It makes them sad. Usually the children miss the parent who does not live with them, and the parent misses the children. Often they try to visit each other frequently. If a parent does not visit the children, it is often because the parent feels very mixed up and sad. When this happens, the children feel even more hurt.

My Name Is _____

The reason I am here is that people care about me. When I come here, I will be learning about marriage, divorce, and remarriage. I will also learn some very important things about myself and how I am special and loved.

This Is a Picture of Me:

My parent who does not live with me does/does not visit me often. That makes me feel _____ because:

Here are some things that I do (or wish that I could do) with my parent who does not live with me:

1.

2.

3.

4.

When a married couple separate from each other, they usually hope to get together again. They may go to a counselor, or "worry doctor," to get help. Sometimes their marriage does get better and they decide to live together again. But sometimes separation does not help, and they decide never to live together again because they don't think they can love each other and be happy together anymore. If they decide this, they may get a divorce, which means they are not married anymore.

When parents get a divorce, it is never their children's fault. But sometimes children think it is. They think that if they had just been better children, or not done naughty things or made so many mistakes, their parents would not have gotten a divorce. This is not true. Everyone makes mistakes, and everyone does naughty things sometimes, even adults. It is never a child's fault if the parents get a divorce. Parents get divorced for lots of reasons, and every couple's reasons are different.

Some reasons why people get divorced are:

1. They don't feel as much in love with each other as they used to. They become disappointed with themselves and each other. Remember, most people decide to get married because they really love each other. It is a great feeling to love and be loved. When these good feelings are gone, both people are very sad.
2. They cannot get along, because they have such different feelings and attitudes. They are not "compatible." When people live together every day, they learn much more about each other than they knew before. If they

disagree about more things than they agree about, they are not "compatible." These people usually fight a lot—usually with words, but sometimes even with hitting.

3. Their needs are not being met. Some people get married because they have certain needs. They might not really love the person they marry, but they get married anyway; maybe so that they won't be lonely anymore, or someone will tell them what to do and when to do it, or for other needs that they have. There are lots of needs that people sometimes get married for. But when people get married because of needs, instead of love, then if one partner or the other changes his or her needs or fails to meet the other's needs, the marriage often falls apart.

4. They want to undo a bad decision. Sometimes people find out that getting married was a big mistake, and no matter how hard they try they cannot seem to work out their problems. Everyone makes mistakes, and divorce is sometimes the only way that a couple can undo the mistake they made when they got married.

5. One partner has a drug or alcohol problem, or both have. When one or both have a drug or alcohol problem, life is very hard for the couple, and often for their children too. Usually the family members get confused, sad, and angry. When one parent drinks or takes drugs a lot, it becomes a really big problem for the family, even though that parent often can't, or won't, see that there is a problem. Sometimes the problem gets so bad that the parents decide to get a divorce.

I think my parents got a divorce because:

Children's lives are changed by their parents' divorce. Some of those changes are for the better, and some are for the worse, but there are always changes.

Because of my parents' divorce, my life has changed in many ways. Some of them are:

1.

2.

3.

4.

5.

6.

2. Divorce and Feelings

When parents get divorced, children have lots of different feelings. Basically there are two kinds. The first kind are the feelings that make us feel good. They are feelings like joy, happiness, love, peacefulness, and relief.

The other kind of feelings make us feel uncomfortable. They are feelings like hurt, fear, anger, guilt, sadness, jealousy, disappointment, confusion, loneliness, and embarrassment. Uncomfortable feelings feel bad, but having them does not make us bad people. Remember, feelings are not right and not wrong; they just are. Everyone has them. It is OK to have feelings, even painful and scary ones. But it is very important not to hold our feelings, especially our uncomfortable ones, inside us, where they can keep hurting us. It helps to talk about them with someone who cares about us. Even though it sometimes hurts to talk about them, it always feels better when we have done it.

Sometimes we have mixed feelings. That's when we have two or more opposite feelings about the same person or event at the same time. Mixed feelings often confuse us so that we don't know how to act. When we have mixed feelings, it is most important to talk about our feelings with someone who cares.

It is very important to pay attention to our feelings, because they can tell us a lot about ourselves. The strength of a feeling is like a thermometer. The stronger it is, the more important it is, and the more it can tell us about ourselves.

Uncomfortable feelings seem to hang around for a long time. The best way to get rid of them is to look at them with someone else's help and try to understand them. For example, let's try to understand *fear.*

Fear is worrying about being hurt or losing something that is very important to us. We can fear physical pain, from cutting our finger, or emotional pain, from failing a test, so that we don't feel happy with ourselves. Fear is an uncomfortable feeling, but it has a very important purpose. It warns us that we might be in some kind of danger, and tells us to pay attention to something. If we feel afraid or nervous, we need to think of what it is we fear losing, or how we could be hurt. Once we decide what it is that is making us fearful, we can do something about it. If I decide that I fear losing my bike when I leave it unlocked in the driveway, then I can go outside and take care of it. If I decide that I fear that a friend will not like me anymore if I do a certain thing, then I can either decide not to do it or talk to my friend about my fear. Sometimes doing something about our fears is hard, and we need some help, that is, we need to talk with someone we trust.

Everyone feels fear sometimes. Most people fear new things, like going to a new school or going to camp for the first time. Most people also fear change. That's because we don't know what to expect, and everyone fears the unknown.

The best way to deal with fear is to begin by admitting to ourselves that we are afraid. Being afraid means only that we are human, not weak. In fact, admitting that we are afraid is a sign of strength. Next we need to decide just what we are afraid of—what it is we might lose, or how we might get hurt. Then we need to do something about our fears. Sometimes that's as simple as locking up our bike, but sometimes it means talking about them with someone who can help. Knowing our fears, the person we talk with can help us to avoid being hurt or losing something that is important to us.

Fear is just one of the uncomfortable feelings. There are many more. The best way to get rid of them is to look at them and try to understand them. Children have many uncomfortable feelings when their parents get divorced.

When my parents got a divorce, I felt:

1.

2.

3.

4.

5.

Now, when I think about their divorce, I feel:

1.

2.

3.

4.

5.

Divorce is never easy for the children or for the adults. However, there are two things that can really help:

1. Remembering that divorce is *never* the fault of the child.

2. Knowing that it takes a long time to get over the uncomfortable feelings that divorce brings.

Before your parent gets remarried, it is important for everyone in the family, especially you, to talk about and try to get rid of as many of those uncomfortable feelings as possible. We are here to help you. You may also find it helpful to talk with your parents, grandparents, or others who can help.

Let's talk about some of the feelings on your list.

3. Something to Do at Home

Our church has a gift for you, a book called *All About Families the Second Time Around,* by Helen Coale Lewis.

Before our next session together, we would like you, your parent, and your almost-stepparent to spend some time reading it, doing the worksheets in it, and talking about it. If you wish, you can also share it with your other parent.

We hope that you will enjoy the time together and learn a lot about one another and what each of you expects from each other in your new family. When you come back next time, bring the book with you so that we can talk about it and how you liked reading it.

4. All About Families the Second Time Around

1. **I like/did not like reading** *All About Families the Second Time Around* **with my parent and almost-stepparent because:**

2. In the beginning, the author talked about lots of words: father, mother, stepmother, stepfather, stepchild, stepbrother, stepsister, half brother, half sister, foster child, orphan, and adopted child. It is very important that you understand what each of these words mean.

   I am still not sure what a _____ is.

3. On one page, you were asked to list all the people in your family. Let's look at that page together.
4. Mrs. Lewis said that what we call our stepparent is important.

   I have decided to call my new stepparent

   _____.

   I decided this because:

5. **My new family will/will not have two last names.**

   I feel _____ about that because:

6. We talked about feelings in our last session, and Mrs. Lewis mentioned in the book how important they are. We hope that you were able to tell your parent(s) and/or stepparent some of your feelings and listen to some of theirs.

   Here are the feelings that I talked about with my parent(s)/stepparent:

7. **They told me that they feel:**

8. Mrs. Lewis had a chart to help you think about the things you like and the things you don't like about each of your parents and stepparents. Let's look at it together.

9. A stepparent can never replace a parent, and should not try to. There are certain things we enjoy doing with each parent and stepparent and with each family that we are part of. Mrs. Lewis gave you a chance to list the things you enjoy doing with each. Let's look at your list together.

10. Our family history is very important to us, as Mrs. Lewis said. Let's look at your list of important things about your first family that you wrote down on the worksheet in the book, and also at what you would like your stepparent to know about you.

11. Did you learn a lot more about your new stepparent and stepbrothers and sisters by listing what you would like to know about them and having them answer your questions?

   The most helpful things I learned were:

12.   Mrs. Lewis talked about not using your parent as a "middleman" when you have questions about your stepparent.

When I think about asking my stepparent ques-

tions about himself/herself, I feel _____
because:

13.   **I think that I play/don't play the "good old days" game when it comes to my family because:**

14.   **I think that** _____ **plays the "good old**

days" game. I feel _____ **about talking**

about it with him/her because:

15. Mrs. Lewis says that love grows between people, and that you should not expect to love your new stepparents instantly. She also says that if you have stepbrothers and sisters, they will probably be loved more by your stepparent than you are because their love has had more time to grow. For the same reason, your parent will probably love you more than your stepbrothers and sisters.

    When I think about this, I feel _____ because:

16. Some children have a hard time because they think that they should be loyal to their natural parents, even if they have a better relationship with their stepparent.

    This is/is not a problem for me because:

17. Do you ever worry about losing some of your parents' love because of the new stepparent? _____ Let's talk about it.

18. Let's look at the list of "special event days" that you made about your family.

    Did you enjoy talking about them with your parent and almost-stepparent?

19. Mrs. Lewis says that new families need new "special event days." Did you think of some for your new family? Let's look at your list of "little special events."

20. Let's look at what you did in the "Write Your Own" part of the book.

21. **The three most helpful things I learned from Mrs. Lewis' book are:**

    1.

    2.

    3.

5. What Now?

We know that preparing for the remarriage of a parent is not easy, and we thank you for the honesty and courage that you have given to completing this workbook and participating in our sessions together. We hope that you have found it helpful, and even fun sometimes. We also hope that you have learned a lot about yourself and your feelings, as well as how to share your feelings in a healthy, helpful way. Finally, we hope most of all that you realize that you are loved and are very important in the life of your parent who is getting married.

Now that we have talked about your feelings about the divorce of your parents and some of the changes and problems that might come up because of this remarriage, the question is "What now?"

We have some suggestions:

1. First, remember what we have learned here so that you can be patient and honest as this new family is being built.

2. Share your ideas and feelings about the wedding ceremony so that it will be a special and important day for you. Then, when the day arrives, do your best, and try your hardest to make it a special day for your whole family.

3. Make a promise to yourself that you will not hold in your feelings or problems, no matter how small or unimportant they may seem. If you would rather not talk to a parent or stepparent, come back to the church or find another friend or counselor. Your parents will probably help you find one if you need one.

4. Be patient! It takes time and work for any family to be healthy and happy. Stepfamilies can take even longer sometimes.

5. Remember that you are loved, and a very important part of this new family.

I feel _____ about the sessions that we have had preparing for remarriage because:

The most helpful thing I learned is:

I do/don't feel a need to talk more about anything else before we plan the wedding ceremony. (If so, what?)

Our thoughts and prayers will be with you and your new family. Thank you for giving us the opportunity to help you prepare for the remarriage of your parent.